YOU HAVE THE *RIGHT* TO REMAIN SILENT
FROM PRISON TO THE PROMISED LAND

YOU HAVE THE *RIGHT* TO REMAIN SILENT
FROM PRISON TO THE PROMISED LAND

VERONIKA JORDAN

TATE PUBLISHING & *Enterprises*

Published by Tate Publishing & Enterprises, LLC
127 E. Trade Center Terrace | Mustang, Oklahoma 73064 USA
1.888.361.9473 | www.tatepublishing.com

Tate Publishing is committed to excellence in the publishing industry. The company reflects the philosophy established by the founders, based on Psalm 68:11,
"The Lord gave the word and great was the company of those who published it."

Book design copyright © 2010 by Tate Publishing, LLC. All rights reserved.
Cover design by Tyler Evans
Interior design by Jeff Fisher

Published in the United States of America

ISBN: 978-1-61566-621-8
1. Biography & Autobiography, Personal Memoirs
2. Religion, Christian Life, Personal Growth
10.02.05

ACKNOWLEDGMENTS

I would like first to thank Joan M. for her patience in reading my first draft.

To Jennifer O., for removing all the "so's" when she read the first three chapters.

To Frances Pasch, for her bubbling personality and welcoming hospitality. For her dedication to her calling to lead new writers to polished and published authors. Fran's poems and devotions are beautiful and inspiring; she is truly our "Paper Missionary."

My unending gratitude to every woman in my writer's group. Rev. Annalee D., Helene K., Claudia J., Pam G., Elaine C., Denise L., Connie C., Sue C., Fran J., Elona H., Cathy S., Nancy S., Dori P., Gigi S., and Nancy B.

To everyone I met at Chestnut Street Community Church, without whom my new life in Christ wouldn't be possible.

To my first Life Group at CSCC. Tracy, Brian, Tom, Gary, Kathleen, Cecile, and Alan.

To my first Bible study friends, Michelle R., Sharon F., Darlene, Damon, Lem, Alexis, Dorothy C., and Kathleen M.

To my special Friday night Christian women's get-together: Sylvia G., Michelle C., Dorothy C., and Dwenette.

To all the women in my present Bible study group: Francene, Gloria, Elona, Joanne, Mary T., Ramona, Mary-Lou, Mary D. and Veronica.

To the hundreds of friends with whom I share the same malady. Annette and Carol for their special friendship and encouragement and for all the crazy times and laughter.

To the ladies from my tennis group who have encouraged me to complete this book.

To Mike F., who introduced me to Boyd Wright, who is an author and gave me some very constructive and helpful insight to polishing my second draft. And to his wife, Jean, for her hospitality.

To my three dearest longtime friends, Judy and Ellie and Sharon, a special thanks for always being there for me.

To Claire, for your insisting I read the book on codependency and for copying the book in its entirety. Thanks for just being there and listening to my complaining and nonsense.

To Greg Tobin, for showing me how to incorporate dialogue into my writing.

To Kathy Miele, for always always always welcoming me and being the sister I never had. Most of all for your love and encouragement.

A special thanks to Denise Loock for the introduction and for your time doing the first proofreading.

A special thanks to Candace K. for making sure all the t's were crossed and the i's dotted.

And a special thanks to Dori Perrucci for doing the final editing.

CONTENTS

FOREWORD

I kept my head bowed over the manuscript our writers' group was editing as I peeked over the top of my glasses at the gray-haired woman seated across from me. Something about the softness of her features and the twinkling humor in her eyes reminded me of the kind-hearted fairy godmother in Disney's® animated *Cinderella*. Yet according to the words we were reading, Veronika was a convicted felon and a recovering alcoholic.

I glanced at her again. *No way,* I thought. *How could this woman, quietly fidgeting with the corner of the paper in front of her, possibly be the person described in this manuscript?*

That was my introduction to the bravely honest woman who tells her story in *You Have the Right to Remain Silent.* The Roni I know bakes cookies and chuckles often. A mischievous grin usually tugs at the corner of her mouth, and her face glows with the joy of Jesus. The Roni I know bears no resemblance to the woman that readers encounter in the early chapters of this book because she's been transformed by the love and grace of God.

2 Corinthians 5:17 says, "Therefore if anyone is in Christ he is a new creation; the old has gone, the new has come" (NIV). As you read this book, you'll witness Roni's miraculous recreation, but more importantly, you'll realize that God is able to transform anyone who's willing to sit still enough and quietly enough to let him do his work.

Roni's story may be a little more dramatic than yours (it's much more dramatic than mine), but the theme of her life story is universal—we all need Jesus. I haven't encountered all the obstacles Roni has faced, but I have battled some of the same enemies—betrayal and rejection, depression and bitterness. And the truth that Roni is discovering on her spiritual journey illuminates my path as well—God walks with us every step of the way.

Roni inspires me, not because of where she's been but because of where she's going—right out into an ugly, scarred world to proclaim that God is in the business of creating masterpieces out of the twisted fragments of our lives.

Turn the page. See the Master Designer at work in one woman's life. You'll want to be next in line.

—Denise K. Loock
Hillsborough, NJ

PROLOGUE

The police officer stormed into Circuit City shouting, "Freeze! You're under arrest!" He pulled my arms behind my back and handcuffed me.

In a matter of minutes, I was escorted out of the store and placed in the backseat of the police car.

I imagined what the gathering audience was thinking. "Oh, look at Miss White Woman in her blue and white tennis dress wearing handcuffs." Some of the faces were compassionate; others puzzled. "What could she have done?"

We pulled away, leaving the crowd perplexed. Living in California, people are never quite sure which scenes are real or which are movie shoots. That day, we were in Pasadena, a beautiful location spot that had turned into an ugly reality. No retakes. This was a wrap.

I had anticipated this moment for a long time.

"I've arrested hundreds of people, but I've never met one like you," the angry officer declared. "You don't seem to have any fear or remorse."

I did not respond because I didn't understand why he was so angry. It was my world that had come to an end. It was my freedom that was being ripped away.

Who would understand the insanity of my life? I didn't look like a common criminal. I got up in the morning like every other mother and took my younger son to school and, from there, drove to the tennis courts at a nearby park. After three sets of doubles, I hopped in the car and headed to Circuit City.

I could best be described as an angry, bitter, and sophisticated thief. God topped the list of candidates I was most angry with. But therein lies the paradox. I didn't believe in God. Still, it became necessary to keep him alive so I'd always have someone to blame for my problems and anguish.

The sound of the police officer's shouting at me broke my reverie. "My wife is going to be furious. I promised her I'd be home by five," he continued to rant. "We're having company for dinner."

"Unlock the cuffs and we can both be on our way home," I mumbled to myself. But I knew that was not an option.

One second less or one minute more would have altered the whole course of events. *If only, if only, if only,* I had waited until the following day.

Why hadn't I run when I saw the police car pull up? Actually, the minute I saw the uniform enter the store, I ran to the area by the pay phones. I ditched my keys in the bottom of the waste basket. The store manger had that little stunt on video.

I was beginning to feel like the patients I used to help prep for surgery. Slowly, the imaginary anesthesia seeped into my veins. Resignation had found that place where even tears couldn't reach.

As we sped through the streets of beautiful Pasadena, I thought of the Rose Bowl parades I had watched on TV. I never dreamed I would someday be arrested a short distance away.

Pulling up to the ramp at the police station, the officer continued his tirade. "What's the deal with the keys?" he asked. "Why did you throw them in the trash can?"

I couldn't tell him the truth. I was terrified he'd search my car. I had checks and falsified documents in the car.

"My son will have to pick up the car," I said. "He doesn't have a key."

"You got kids home lady, and you're out here stealing?"

"You have no idea who I am or why I did what I did. I am so consumed with fear right now that there is no room for remorse. I have two teenage sons who will be forced to live alone and care for themselves. The older one is gravely ill."

He never did respond to that.

In his haste to get home, he broke procedure and didn't search my car.

That neglect reduced my sentence by a few years.

IN THE BEGINNING

"Strict Irish Catholic" would have made for a great sit-com. *The Addams Family* and the *Munsters* had nothing on us.

Mom was the innocent and fragile one; Dad was the military officer issuing orders and edicts, and the children jumping at the mere sound of his voice. No, my father was never in the military service. I'm guessing it was a latent desire.

I'm not quite sure at what age I learned there were Ten Commandments. I only knew about the fourth one. "Honor thy father and thy mother" became my mantra. We surely knew the fear of God, and if we dared to disobey Mom and Dad, we were committing a sin and going to *that* place. Our religion taught us a humorless devotion to God.

Dinnertime was no fun. "Wipe that smile off your face," my father barked. On other occasions, when I sat with a serious expression, he would ask, "What's that puss for?"

I never knew what face to wear. By the age of twenty, I had learned so many expressions and behaviors I could have won an Academy Award for the role of *Sybil*.

I remember something the humorist Erma Bombeck had said about uptight joylessness as she described a small child who was sitting in church one Sunday. He kept turning around and smiling at everyone. Suddenly, his mother jerked him around and in a loud whisper said, "Stop that grinning! You're in church!" Erma said she was tempted to grab the child with the tear-stained face and tell him about her God. The happy God. The smiling God. If we couldn't smile in church, where could we smile?

In our family, we couldn't smile in church or at the dining room table.

I was the little girl who was afraid of the inside of a church, the fear it instilled in me by parents like mine, and the punishing God they chose to threaten me with.

In first grade, our family moved from Newark to Union. Two months later, my brother Todd was born. Three years later, my brother Dennis arrived. I still have the letter I wrote to my mother: "How do you like the new baby, Mom? Dad said he's cute. I hope so. Well, I wanted a sister, but I will have to accept whatever God sends us." Can't you just picture the halo above this precious daughter?

Now I was caught between two baby brothers and the perfect firstborn son.

Everything in my life was overshadowed by my parents' favoritism toward Patrick. He was three years older than me. Every day I lived in that house, I knew I was not as good as Patrick. I couldn't blame him. From the stories I've been told, Patrick was very sickly as an infant.

He was in the hospital with pneumonia for weeks after he was born. At two, he had to have a hernia operation. I believe my mother was very protective of him because of his illnesses. Patrick's natural behavior was easygoing. However, as a young child, I didn't see him that way. All I knew was he was the "goodie two shoes."

Patrick was the fair-haired blond, blue-eyed child. When he was three, he modeled for a magazine. I can still recall looking at those pictures and hearing my mother tell her friends, "I couldn't continue to take the bus all the way into Newark after Roni was born." I hated her insinuation that I was to blame for ruining his modeling career.

By the age of seven, I think I wore a hole in the corner of the dining room carpet. That was the primary punishment for years, being made to stand in the corner with my face to the wall. Whether it was two minutes or ten, it didn't matter. To a young child, it seemed like an eternity.

When I think back to the things that prompted punishment, they seem so absurd and silly. Jumping on the bed, throwing pillows around, or turning the radio on. I remember sitting at the table for an hour with a bowl of cold oatmeal and being forced to eat it. As an adult I skip breakfast; the thoughts of it make me nauseous.

One of the actions that often put me in the corner was talking when I went to bed. Patrick and I shared the same bedroom, and I can still recall the times my father would be yelling at me to stop talking.

The more desperate I became for attention, the worse my behavior got. My grades suffered. More punishments! Now I was being sent to my room for hours, not being allowed to play dodgeball with the neighborhood kids after school. The constant reminders of Patrick's perfect grades! The vicious cycle! I was too young to understand my behavior would never bring about the attention I needed and wanted. *I love you,* the three most important words for a child, I would never hear.

"Oh, you can't be Patrick Brennan's sister," the nuns would say. This little brat, related to the angelic, intelligent, and perfect Patrick? How was that possible?

Hey, Sister Mary Ellen Patricia Catherine Elizabeth of the Holy Whatever, didn't you ever hear, all things are possible with God?

Before I even graduated from grammar school, my parents had me enrolled in an all girls' Catholic high school. I felt violated. I wanted to remain with my friends from grammar school. I had been with them for eight years. Back that many years ago, you were never included in decision making. Okay, yes, I was mischievous, but not a bad child. To me, it was another form of authority, proving to me that they had the power to make me do what they wanted.

I'd had a childhood devoid of nurturing, touching, or hugging. Forget extracurricular activities or sports. There were a few dance lessons. No music lessons. Grades were the only thing that mattered.

When you're that young, you don't realize how important all these things are. I had two baby brothers at home. My mother was too busy to continue to take me to dance classes. My friends were participating in all these fun activities. I tagged along with one who became a gymnast. I saw many of these sports being played through my friends.

It's funny the things you recall as you get older. My father never had any interest in sports. None of my brothers participated in Little League or the like. Yet I remember attending a Dodgers game in New York with my dad when I was in my teens.

Both of my parents were very serious. Living in this environment led me to seek excitement outside the home. Just sipping a cherry Coke in the corner drugstore was fun. Lying became a way of life. I had to go to the library to do reports. Of course, my father would drive me there, and I'd go into the library. Five minutes later, I escaped to meet with my friends and hang out. I envied friends who were allowed to wear jeans and ballerina slippers, while I had my uniform and brown oxfords on. I wanted to wear my hair in a ponytail. Even something as normal as that wasn't allowed. Until I graduated from high school, my mother insisted that my hair be kept short.

Babysitting provided an escape. I didn't have to lie about it. It got me out of the house weeknights. And it gave me the freedom to make phone calls and of course to smoke.

In June 1960 my high school graduation was the happiest day of my young life. I immediately went to work as a key-punch operator at the phone company and was thrilled with my newfound freedom.

Patrick entered the seminary, which was the pinnacle of my Irish Catholic parents' dream.

A lot of animosity flowed between my mother and me during these years.

She hated the fact that I was out every night. That was the thing during that era. We found a different place to hang out and dance for almost every night of the week. None of my friends drank. I never did either. I was also dating a Jewish fellow from work by the name of Ira.

He was about eight years older than me. A few nights he would meet me at one of the clubs. However, he had recently divorced. I knew there wouldn't be any future with him. That would have been grounds for annihilation in my Catholic family's view.

I continued to live at home. My mother finally gave up the nightly vigil of waiting up until I got home.

Shortly before my twentieth birthday, a few of my friends and I went on a ski-trip to Lake George in New York. We were having a blast. Out skiing all day and sitting by the fire in the evening. Around the fourth day, a few of us left the motel room together and were walking to a nearby restaurant for dinner. Suddenly, the unexpected happened, and I found myself sitting on the ground. I had slipped on a patch of ice. There was no doctor around or even in close proximity to the hotel. I made it through the night with an ice pack on it. The following morning, I boarded the bus to the ski lodge, and, after depositing the entire busload of people, the driver took me to see a doctor.

I arrived home very late that evening in a cast and with the aid of crutches. Two months later, it was discovered that I had a fractured kneecap. It was during my recuperation following surgery that my parents met Ira for the first time when he came to visit me. He was mature, good-looking, and very well-mannered. My parents were impressed with his visiting me and his concern. And added to the mix was the bouquet of roses he carried in with him. They really liked him.

We continued to date for another year, during which time my parents were sure they would have a Jewish son-in-law. It was kind of humorous given the fact that neither Ira nor I ever discussed marriage. I never did tell my parents that he was divorced and had a young daughter.

At twenty-two, I met Brad, my husband-to-be. I continued to see Ira for a short time. But once things became serious with Brad, I broke off with Ira. He and I remained good friends because we worked together.

My mother was devastated when Ira and I broke up. Brad was a great guy. He was also a motorcyclist. In fact, that's how our relationship began. I loved to ride on motorcycles. He was always so polite to my parents. At that time my mother was recuperating from gall bladder surgery, and he'd come in and ask her how she was feeling. My parents would have died if they had any inkling that he had a motorcycle or that their daughter rode on the back of it.

Brad was very understanding and didn't want me to get in trouble. He lived about twenty minutes away, but he never complained about picking me up in his car and then going back to his house to get the bike. We repeated the process at the end of the evening. Those were the days when your date came to your door and rang the bell. They were also the days when your date walked you up to the door at the end of the evening.

Brad and I were engaged a few months later. When I showed my mother the ring, she went into a rage and didn't speak a word to me for a month. We were the perfect mother and daughter duo: *engaged and enraged!*

My parents either liked you or they disliked you. There was never any middle ground. Like most things, I couldn't quite grasp what the reasoning was behind their thinking. My mother influenced my dad to a great extent. I honestly don't believe my father really cared which one I married. I am confident that if I had stopped seeing

Brad and went back with Ira my mother would have found fault with that too.

On June 4, 1966, Brad and I were married. During the reception my father went up to his new son-in-law and said, "Well, she's all yours now." He was rid of the disobedient daughter.

Two years later, my brother Patrick was ordained. He seemed more relaxed now. For the first time, I came to appreciate his sense of humor, and the bantering between us grew routine. Of course, I never let him forget he was the favorite child.

The following year, Brad and I bought our first home. A short time later, I became pregnant with our first son, Chad. For the following three years, I continued to turn myself inside out to please my parents. We had them over for dinners and visited with them frequently.

My mother-in-law couldn't have been more awed with her first grandson and her obvious delight at being called "Grandma."

I often wished my mother-in-law was my mother. I've always admired people who accepted you just for being you. I never once heard her criticize anyone. No matter what we did she was always elated. She was thrilled when we bought the house. She'd stop over and visit. She was so different from my mother. I didn't have to have the house spotless to please her.

My in-laws owned their own diner. She'd bring over cold cuts and salads on a whim. It was great. She was just so comforting.

She had many siblings, and they and their spouses loved to play poker. That became a monthly night of fun. We only played with nickels and dimes. We had a ball.

My family never did anything like that. Everything was regimented in the Brennan house. Dinner exactly at 6 p.m. We never did anything relaxing. I don't think we ever as a family watched television. Well, that's not exactly true. We were made to sit in front of the television every week when Bishop Sheen was on. And my father would actually drill us afterwards with questions.

In 1968 my brother Todd moved to Colorado. Dennis had joined the Marines. Both had made these drastic moves for the sole purpose of getting away from Mom and Dad.

My mother never worked after she and my father got married. For twenty-five years, she was home. Her life consisted of making beds, baking, and preparing for dinner. Her world revolved around her kids. With Todd and Dennis gone and Patrick living away from home, all she had left to obsess about was me. Now that I had a baby and was no longer working, she became overbearing. At least once a week, she would visit with one of her friends, and I'd have to make lunch and entertain them. Then, of course, we had to go there for dinner every Sunday.

I was in a bowling league on Tuesdays. That worked for both of us. Mom got to babysit, and I had some free time. But the catch was that I had to stay for dinner. And Brad would meet us there. It would have been nice if staying for dinner had been optional. That's where our greatest differences were. Everything had to be done the way the Brennans wanted it done. There was never the slightest bit of flexibility. I could not say, "Hey, Mom, Brad won't be joining us for dinner." Nor would I dare say, "Listen, Mom, I'm tired and would rather go home after bowling."

In 1973 I gave birth to our second son, Eric.

Nothing changed, and we continued the Sunday ritual of going to my parents for dinner. And we'd have to wait until Patrick arrived before dinner could be served. I really was blessed to have the husband I did. He would have much preferred to stay home on his one day off and watch football or baseball. But no, we had to go to Mom's for dinner.

It didn't seem to matter how much time we spent together. My mother had to know everything that was going on. Without fail the phone would ring every day and she'd want to know how everything was. I couldn't handle it after a few months and I finally took the phone off the hook. Unfortunately, that only meant a call first thing the following morning, wanting to know where I was. Why didn't I answer the phone? There were no answering machines at the time or voice mail service, which meant she kept calling until I answered.

If I told her I was visiting a friend, she'd immediately want to know who then tell me I spent too much time away from home.

In the summer of 1975, we visited my brother Todd in Colorado. We rented a small Scotty tagalong and drove cross-country with the kids. Those two weeks proved to be most adventuresome, leaving us with memories of driving through the clouds at the top of Pike's Peak, panning for gold, and watching streams of bills being printed at the U.S. Mint in Denver.

We could sleep as late as we wanted. We could skip breakfast. I could wear jeans and t-shirts. There was a wonderful sense of freedom being outdoors. We camped out at Estes Park. But for me just being away from my mother gave me the greatest freedom. My brother didn't have a phone or television.

Brad and I took a trip to California during the summer of 1977.

We had dropped a few hints that we would love to live in California. So my mother knew immediately when we told her we were taking a trip out there it was more than a sightseeing visit. My mother could be very spiteful, and I guess she thought by refusing to take care of my kids we wouldn't go. She never thought my mother-in-law would agree to stay home from work for ten days to care for the kids. Meanwhile, Irene was thrilled to have the opportunity to be with them for that length of time.

We did the usual sightseeing. However, the main purpose for the trip was to check out different locations. We stayed with a friend Brad had gone to high school with. He and his wife showed us around Orange County and Los Angeles. I visited the medical college in Los Angeles that I was planning to attend.

This was long before computers did all the work for us. We visited the Chamber of Commerce. We checked out the Yellow Page listings of alarm companies. That was the type of work my husband had been doing since we got married.

The warm weather and sunny skies had great appeal, and moving away from Helen and Francis, my parents, made our decision easy.

One year later our house was sold. We had the closing on September 1, 1978. We had sold most of our furniture, what we kept was already in the Hertz rental truck. On Sept. 2nd we left for California with the car in tow, two kids, two hamsters, and Gidget, the poodle, all in the front seat of the truck. It took us 13 days to reach the "Land of the Rich and Famous."

The first year was wonderful. Brad worked for Honeywell installing fire and burglar alarms. I returned to college to complete the courses needed to get my LVN degree to work in California. A short time later, I started working at a hospital in Los Angeles. We even bought a home.

I soon learned, however, that three thousand miles would not give me the peace of mind I had hoped for.

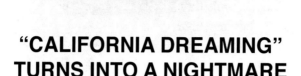

"CALIFORNIA DREAMING"
TURNS INTO A NIGHTMARE

Despite the distance, there were still the weekly calls, questionnaire letters, and criticism.

The first four years, my parents came to visit four times, and we rolled the red carpet out every time. Patrick accompanied them three times. Brad and I used our vacation time to take them to every tourist attraction in southern California: a private tour of Warner Brothers, the Magic Castle, which is a very exclusive private club, every museum in Los Angeles, the Huntington Gardens and Library in Pasadena, Sea World in San Diego, Universal Studios in Burbank, and Magic Mountain in Valencia. Todd came twice, and Dennis, who had married during this time, visited with his new wife, Carol.

The first few years were difficult. Brad worked long hours. I had to be in work at 6:30 a.m. and was home by 4 p.m. Most nights, Brad didn't get home until 7 or 8 p.m. When Chad was old enough, we signed him up in Little

League. That's when things changed and our social life improved.

Brad made friends at his job, and we started going out for dinner and shows. Eric also joined Little League. It took another few years before we really felt comfortable in California. Unfortunately, neither of our salaries matched the friends we became involved with. Next thing you know, we joined a rather exclusive tennis club. That meant lessons and nice tennis outfits and more socializing. By this time, the kids were old enough to be left alone for a few hours.

Next thing you know, we're looking for a bigger house. My reasoning was so we could be closer to the hospital where I worked. I was on call one night a week and one weekend a month. It only took another year before the reality set in and we were falling behind in our mortgage payments. We were hosting expensive dinners and throwing parties.

Our credit cards were maxed out. We got a second mortgage, but even that didn't help. A year later, we were on every bill collector's list, and our home went into foreclosure. Along with his full-time job, Brad did a lot of side jobs for friends or referrals. I was stunned when the day came and he said, "I'm sorry, Roni, I can't keep up this pace anymore! There's no end to your demands. Every time I do another job and get us out of the hole, you spend more money and put us right back in the red. I'm finished."

Brad's quiet and easygoing nature always hid what was going on in his mind. I had no idea he felt this way. He had worked so hard all those years. It was only a matter of months before the house went into foreclosure. He started drinking, and that would take our marriage to a shocking and vicious end.

This wonderful guy had worshipped the ground upon which I walked. This wonderful father idolized his sons. He took them rock-climbing, camping, fishing. He helped at their baseball games. And all I did was pressure him to work more hours, make more money, and then take time off to entertain my family and their friends.

I remember the day my mother made her weekly phone call and I broke down telling her that we had started to pack up our belongings and were moving them into a storage unit. She and my dad were leaving the following day for Ireland. I knew nothing about the trip prior to this conversation. A large group was traveling from Patrick's church. She left for her vacation all upset over our situation.

This was a perfect example of our problem. It just wasn't possible to hide what was going on. Oftentimes I would do all I could to avoid telling her any details. But she would hound me with questions. And I'd fall into the trap of revealing much more than I should have.

Five days before we had to be out of the house, Brad found an apartment for us. But his drinking was out of hand, and he was not coming home some nights. The kids were devastated, and I was at a loss as to what to do.

I thought for sure when I told my mother about this she would at least show a little empathy. I almost went into cardiac arrest when she responded with the following:

"Well, Roni, what did you expect? I heard you nagging him. You should be more understanding of his drinking problem." Across three thousand miles, I was still being criticized. I wanted to scream at her and let her know the nagging she heard was because I expected him to take off work while they were visiting. I nagged him to go grocery shopping for a few items I had overlooked when preparing dinners for them. I nagged him to come home early because my parents were there.

Exhausted, depressed, and distraught, I could no longer function. I was incapable of accepting my mother's callous response or the reality that we no longer had a place to live. Everything had to be put in storage. In August of 1985 I underwent surgery for an obstruction in my throat. It wasn't a major operation. However, it kept me from returning to work for several months. My disability benefits were coming to an end. Everything was happening so fast.

I woke up in the morning and hoped things would miraculously change. But instead, I woke up facing more and more turmoil, knowing I was in no condition to return to my job in the operating room. I could never have concentrated long enough to keep my thoughts focused on the task of rapidly handing the surgeon the correct instrument. Added to all this was my inability to accept that our marriage was coming to an end.

In October, one month after moving into the apartment, our car was repossessed.

My first arrest took place during those few months we were in the apartment. However, that wasn't for any intentional wrongdoing. I had a gotten a ticket months prior for going through a stop sign. And of course I ignored it. I knew nothing about citations or tickets or appearing in court. I was shocked when I got pulled over and was told there was a warrant out for me for failure to appear in court. A friend of mine came and put up the bail of $500 for me, and I was released at 4 a.m.

Brad's drinking escalated. I had no compassion or understanding of his problem. I felt only rage that some liquid in a bottle could stop my husband from caring about his family. Each day, the nightmare worsened.

In January 1986, after four months of living in the apartment, we were evicted. For the next year, we lived at a campground in the only thing we still owned: a thirteen foot tagalong trailer.

One thing I learned was making friends was not easy. California is a transient state. I don't think we met more than a dozen true natives all the time we lived there. You don't develop relationships that easily. We had a lot of acquaintances. When my husband turned forty, a couple we knew threw a surprise party for him. There were about fifty people there. These were people from the tennis club, some we had met through little league, and others from our jobs. However, when things started to fall apart, we lost our membership to the club, and the boys were finished with little league. And of course we didn't have a phone in the trailer. I continued to see a few friends, but after the first arrest, it was just too embarrassing to keep in contact with these people.

I found a box of checks in my husband's truck. The account had been closed, but being desperate, I used them to get food and other necessities. I continued using them for months. As things worsened my activities escalated. I was purchasing items that could be returned for cash. I was in a drugstore one day attempting to return an item and the store manager became suspicious and had the security guard escort me to his office, where I was held until the police arrived. That's when I found out that using these checks was forgery. And so that was my second arrest. Three days later, my husband bailed me out. I was put on probation for a year.

My son Chad, who was sixteen, became very sick and was diagnosed with ulcerative colitis. For three years, he lived with excruciating pain when the disease flared up. He went on Medicaid and was hospitalized for a few weeks. The insanity intensified, and I became more and more bitter.

I had borrowed money from a friend so that Chad and I would have one night in a motel room. It was Fourth of July, and Chad wanted so much to be with his friends at the fireworks, but I didn't have enough gas in my car to drive him there. Instead, he was lying on the bed watching TV, groaning about how hungry he was. We were into our third day without eating. I couldn't listen to him any longer.

I walked to the nearest restaurant and asked the young fellow working behind the counter if he would please give me one meal. I quickly explained my desperation. He told me I would have to ask the manager.

When the manager appeared, I begged him for just one meal or even a hamburger. "My son hasn't eaten in a few days."

"We're about to close. Everything's put away."

"But I promise to come back tomorrow and wash dishes."

"Sorry, I can't."

I walked out in tears as he locked the door behind me and put up the closed sign.

My tears turned to sobs as I stared at the wasted food brimming over the sides of the dumpster. Five minutes later, I had to look my son in the face and tell him, "Sorry, Chad, I couldn't get you anything to eat."

Eric had already flown back to New Jersey when school let out in June. My parents had invited him to stay with them for a *few* weeks. Circumstances had devastated both of my sons. The decision to visit my parents was best. At the end of July I called my mother and asked that he be sent home. Three weeks later I called her, *again*. Her refusal to acknowledge my wishes enraged me.

Ten days later, Eric called me. "I want to come home, but they won't let me. Grandma enrolled me in *school* here."

"Please be patient for a while longer," I said.

My mother's disrespect of my rights to have my son with me was causing an internal volcano to bubble. Yet I could do nothing to breach the miles that separated Eric and me.

Two months later came the sobs. "Mom, please come and get me. I overheard Grandma on the phone with your cousin Patty. They're talking about putting me in foster care."

That was the straw that broke the camel's back.

During the time we were living at the trailer park, our mail was still being delivered to our previous apartment. Once a week, I would return to get the mail. In the mailbox was an envelope that obviously had a credit card in it. It was not sent to us; it was delivered in error. I held on to it for a few weeks, and it became my ace in the hole. I knew it was wrong to even consider using it, but at that point, it became necessary.

I was so filled with anger that I no longer cared about my actions or the consequences. I had to get a ticket and get to New Jersey. I called and ordered a ticket by phone using that credit card. This was long before personal identification numbers, e-tickets, and having to show identification. The ticket was waiting at the counter when I arrived at the airport. This would be the beginning of my conniving and of discovering new ways of getting money and other things we needed.

By nine the following evening, I was heading for New Jersey, via a stolen airline ticket.

I only planned to be gone for a week or two and prayed that Chad would be all right during this time. With the credit card, I was able to withdraw cash from an ATM. I then rented a motel room for one month so Chad would have someplace to stay. I would put the trailer up for sale when I returned. Unbeknownst to me, my husband was now living with his girlfriend. I did contact him at work, and he agreed to keep an eye on Chad and make sure he had his dinner and a ride to school.

Upon my arrival in New Jersey, I went directly to my mother-in-law's and unpacked.

My mother-in-law had called my parents and told them she'd like to take Eric to his cousin's birthday party that evening. She picked Eric up around 7 p.m. They were not very happy about letting him go on a school night, but they couldn't flat out refuse her. I will never forget the expression on his face when he arrived back at her house and saw me there. It's one of those moments I will treasure forever. He was so excited, and he was crying and I was crying. For the first time in many months, he had hope of returning with me to California.

The following weeks were torture for me. I couldn't conceive of how to get Eric away from my parents. I didn't even let them know I was in New Jersey until the third week.

They acted as if Eric was their own child and I had no rights to see him. It was horrible.

I would pick him up Saturday afternoons, but I was told he had to be home by 9 p.m. He had to go to church with them early Sunday morning.

I tried to make the best of it. I'd take him out to dinner or a movie. One day I took Eric and his two cousins with us on a tour of NBC. They were thrilled. It was the first time either of them had been through the Lincoln Tunnel. One Sunday Eric and I drove into New York and went to the Empire State Building. Afterwards we walked to Rockefeller Center. It was early December, and we were watching the people ice skate, and Eric wanted so much to ice skate. I called my dad and told him we'd be late getting back. He went crazy.

"You get him back here right now. What are you doing in New York when he has to go to school in the morning?"

I hated him at that moment. It was only eight o'clock. It broke my heart to have to say to Eric, "Sorry, you can't go ice skating; Grandpa wants you back there immediately."

I remember walking him to the door that night and both my mother and father were waiting at the door. I can't recall what my father was saying, but it wasn't very nice and definitely not warranted. Whatever it was it upset Eric. He was crying that he wanted to be with me. They wouldn't even let me in the door. This screaming took place in front of the house.

I felt like I was being split in half. I had to get back to California. It was gut-wrenching knowing Chad was in the motel alone. And it was even more gut-wrenching to be present to watch these other scenes with my parents.

I knew I couldn't take this much longer. I was sending money back to my other son to pay for the motel. My husband was taking him to school and making sure he was fed. But he was still drinking and oftentimes didn't pick Chad up after school. Chad would go to his friends and then walk home, which was a few miles. And yet I didn't have the money to get two tickets back to California.

I had been working with my mother-in-law in a small restaurant. I worked the breakfast shift, and that gave me some pocket money.

By Christmas school break, I was ready to commit myself to the nearest psych ward. Eric was a basket case. When I went to pick him up from school, the principal called my parents.

"Do not let Eric leave with his mother," my father told him. "I'm on my way to pick him up myself."

I was livid. I drove back to my parents' home and waited outside. When my father pulled up, I took Eric.

I knew I was acting impulsively, and there was no question that my behavior was wrong. However, I could no longer listen to the criticism and putdowns. I had always been a responsible parent, and unfortunately, things had gone very wrong that year. My parents' increasing superiority had pushed me to the limit.

Kids want to be with their birth mother even when things aren't stable and secure. In this situation, the difficulty had never been about abuse. This was about a situation that couldn't be predicted and one that turned bad so rapidly that I didn't know how to handle it. I didn't know if I could make things right, but I did know being belittled and accused of things that weren't true was not going to make the situation right.

For all the discord, Christmas turned out to be fun. Brad flew in with Chad, and we had dinner at Irene's and visited some of her relatives and some of my old friends. I did go visit my parents. I wouldn't deprive Chad from seeing his grandparents.

Little would I know that I was a week away from another big loss. Chad and Brad flew back to California immediately after Christmas. My mother-in-law had paid for their trip.

A few days after Christmas, I called the storage place where we had all our belongings. I wanted to make sure the payment was current. My husband had been paying the monthly fee and promised he would continue doing so.

"Sorry, Mrs. Jordan, your unit is vacant. We sold all your belongings at auction. Your contract stated this would happen if you were two months behind in your payments."

I was numb. I was hysterical. My mother-in-law had to give me a drink to calm me down. I couldn't handle this. Everything I owned was gone in one day. All our clothes. Washer and dryer. Television. All the boys' personal stuff. Living room furniture. Dining room furniture. Three sets of bedroom furniture. The list goes on and on. How would I ever recoup from this? This was my very last hope. It was my intention when I returned to California to put an ad in the paper and sell as much as possible. Now it was gone. I had absolutely nothing.

I went into a local bar that evening and drank myself into oblivion and stole someone's credit card.

That credit card was our ticket home.

A few days later my mother called wanting to know when I would be bringing Eric back. She reminded me school would be starting right after New Year's Day.

"I'm not bringing him back. We're going back to California immediately."

I left New Jersey in a very angry state of mind and with a determination to turn this situation around at whatever cost.

LIFE OF CRIME BEGINS

Upon my return to California, Chad, Eric, and I continued to live in the motel. I made a promise to them that we would get through this together and that I would find a way to replace all we had lost.

Returning to work seemed to be the obvious path to take. But this was no longer a situation of working to pay the bills. To accomplish what needed to be done would be comparable to climbing out of the Grand Canyon in a week. There was no easy or even feasible way that a paycheck would cover the necessary security deposit plus rent, utilities, food, furniture, refrigerator, and everything else that was considered a necessity.

I immediately applied for welfare. I still had pipe dreams of my husband pulling himself together so things would return to normal. I was exhausted from all the months of struggling to pay for the motel room, along with food and other necessities, plus worrying about Chad.

Brad contributed some money toward the cost of the motel room.

The kids would have nothing to do with him. Both boys were furious at their father. Furious doesn't really come close to how they felt. Angry, bitter, and every other adjective you could think of. Chad was especially affected. He had worked to buy his own stereo and several other items he treasured. He blamed his father for so many things: living in a motel room, his mother out stealing to pay for the room and buy food, no longer owning one single thing, and added to the mix his father was now living with some other woman and spending money to get drunk every night.

People who have never experienced hard times or sudden misfortunes don't have a clue the conundrum one meets at the forks in the roads. Yes, I qualified for welfare, which paid for one month's rent. However, unless I could prove a permanent place of residency at the end of thirty days, I could no longer receive any money.

Where could I find a place to live with only $500 to cover the security deposit and first and last month's rent in advance? How could I even qualify to get an apartment when my credit was bad, and I had a bankruptcy among the list of outstanding debt, and was unemployed?

There were times I wished I could succumb to the insanity of my situation. Maybe succumb is not exactly the right word. I can't even describe the torment that plagued me every waking moment. I didn't even know what a full night's sleep was like. Every morning heaped more pain on top of more pain. I couldn't stand watching the kids suffer. I lived in constant fear of getting caught. What would happen to them if I wasn't there providing for them? There were times I wished for the courage to swallow a bottle of pills. But I wouldn't in a million years abandon my kids, not after what I went through with my family. I just wanted some relief. I would have settled for a twenty-four-hour reprieve. Anything.

My father-in-law passed away in April. My mother-in-law had offered to send us $5,000 that she had received from his insurance. However, there was one stipulation. The money could only be used to get us an apartment and that her son was to live with us. Consequently, Brad and I agreed to try again, and we found a very nice three-bedroom apartment for $750 a month. I forged several documents in order to get a driver's license under my maiden name. The foreclosure had left us out of the loop for credit under our family name.

It took twelve months to furnish the entire apartment and replace all that we had lost: new refrigerator, stereo, television, computer, microwave, and more. Every bit of food we ate, every stitch of clothing we wore, even the car I drove, along with the rent, was paid for with bad checks and fake credit. My nights were spent planning and scheming how I could get money.

Brad was still working at the alarm company. He was contributing to the rent and coming home every night, even though most nights it was well after midnight or when the bars closed.

When I began to scheme and plan to do things that are illegal, it's mind-boggling how chaotic things get. It's like the domino effect. I'd manage to keep the third and fourth domino up, but then the sixth and seventh would go down. I was constantly picking them up only to have them go down again and again. I did get a job working in a doctor's office. Since I was now reporting to a probation officer, I had to be working and I had to use my real name, but I couldn't use my current address since that was under another name. Keeping things straight became very difficult.

Most of my forays consisted of forging credit card applications at major appliance stores, furniture stores, computer stores, and department stores. I could walk into any of the above and within the hour be approved for amounts as high as $3,000 to $15,000. And every time I entered another store, I was using a fictitious name. I'm not kidding when I say I sometimes couldn't remember who I was supposed to be.

All it cost me was $10 to get my picture taken in any check cashing place, and within twenty minutes, I had an official California Identification Card all neatly laminated.

Following that, I'd go to the Department of Motor Vehicles and apply for a driver's permit to match the ID card. There were times I had managed to get enough information on a real person's background and go to the DMV where I could get a temporary license.

I don't think at the time there was a label for this type of theft. Today, it is known as identity theft and has become a major problem.

With this type of identification, I would open up checking accounts for as little as a few hundred dollars and, a week later, pick up a box of checks at the bank. Back then, it took as long as two weeks for checks to clear. That gave me more than enough time to buy the food we needed and clothes for the kids.

I would purchase several hundred dollars worth of items then spend the next week returning them in small increments. Anything under $100 did not require a receipt. I would spend all day doing this. I was missing so many days from work that I finally was terminated. I really didn't care. I wasn't making nearly enough to cover any expenses.

So much time had passed that it just became routine. I knew from day one what I was doing was wrong. When you're angry and desperate, you just stop caring and do what you have to do. And as each day passes, your anger grows. In time, the anger grew into rage. You don't know how to get out of it. It truly becomes survival of the fittest.

Brad knew what I was doing. But he didn't care. He wasn't about to sacrifice any more of his drinking money than he had to.

The boys also knew what I was doing. But they also understood that my actions provided for them.

Chad was having severe flare-ups from the ulcerative colitis and was in a lot of pain. There wasn't one specialist who would accept Medicaid. There was one hospital that wouldn't even treat him during an emergency situation. It was so hard to keep my rage in check. I was frustrated, angry, and being forced to watch my son suffer, and I could do so little to help.

I had lost contact with my entire family. Yes, that was by choice, but little by little, I lost all contact with friends. I couldn't tell them what I was doing. It's humiliating never to have money and allow friends to witness this insanity. The closest I can come to describing my life was to say it was like being catapulted into another dimension or landing on Mars.

I managed to save up enough cash to take Chad to see a specialist. The test results confirmed that the ulcerative colitis was quite advanced. Prednisone helped for a few months, but the next flare-up came on him with a vengeance. He had severe abdominal pain and constant diarrhea. And the bleeding was profuse. He was admitted to the hospital immediately and remained on a TPN (Total Parenteral Nutrition) regimen, which is administered intravenously for ten days. And all he was allowed to eat were ice chips. After his discharge, he remained on the prednisone and a very restricted diet with no milk products.

He was feeling better, but the bleeding and diarrhea continued. Not as severe, but certainly enough to be worrisome.

My husband and I continued to share the apartment, but we could not be in each other's presence without fighting. He truly was a functional alcoholic; every night was spent in the bar, but he never missed a day from work.

My mother-in-law, Irene, moved to California in August of 1988. I had always had a good relationship with her. The boys and I thought that if she lived with us Brad would come to his senses and he'd start coming home after work. Unfortunately, that never happened. Her presence there exacerbated the problem.

She would never criticize anything he did. And she wasn't about to admit he had a drinking problem. She got a part-time job to help cover the rent money. This further enabled him to drink more and care less knowing Mom would cover for him.

The situation became explosive. The kids were angry that she couldn't do more to make her son come home. The arguing and screaming was horrible. That continued for months, and I finally decided to get my own apartment. The marriage was over.

I moved out sometime in October of 1989, and Eric came with me. Chad remained with his grandmother and father.

The more frenzied each new day became, the more normal each passing day appeared. I accepted it as a way of life. To add to this insane routine was my need to play tennis as often as possible in the early morning hours. It was the only thing that resembled something close to normal. It became my only reason to get out of bed. It became the energizer I needed to go forth every day and do the things that needed to be done.

The women I played with were not friends. They were acquaintances I had been playing tennis with for years on the courts at a nearby park. It didn't cost me a penny and yet helped me to hold on to one normal activity. It allowed me two hours to forget the horror I would face when I left the courts.

Shortly before Christmas I met Andre. He was tall, dark, and handsome. We dated for a few months before we realized there was twenty years difference between us. The trend was quite popular: the older woman and the younger guy. We were the Victoria Principal and Andy Gibb of the San Fernando Valley, minus the money and notoriety.

Chad had spent Thanksgiving and Christmas with Eric and me. With a stolen credit card, I managed to get all new Christmas decorations and a live tree. It was a very plentiful holiday.

The whole month of January was very peaceful. Andre came over a few times a week. He and Eric would spend hours playing Nintendo along with all the other video games. The three of us went ice skating together, and we even played tennis a few times. I felt like I now had three sons.

Chad was still living with his father and his grand-mother. Fortunately he had a large bedroom. It had been a bachelor apartment prior to our moving there. The land-lord had converted into a third bedroom, so Chad had his own entrance. He pretty much came and went on his own. Brad seldom came home. Irene was still working part time, and she made all of Chad's meals.

Eric and I would go over for dinner a few times a week. She knew everything that was going on. She knew what I was doing. Not the details. She just accepted every-thing as though it was a normal, everyday occurrence.

January was the peace before February's storm.

And then Valentine's Day arrived, the perfect reason to go out and steal more things to give the kids. My never-ending guilt drove me to these "Journeys of Replacement." Every possible chance I got I would be replacing some-thing of value the boys had lost. It hurt so much to see them suffering. Chad was still suffering physically. Emo-tionally he was devastated with all that was going on. On more than one occasion he had physically assaulted his father. I have to say with all I'd been through this was the one action that terrified me the most.

He was such a good kid. I thank God Brad never fought back. He would never hurt the boys in any way that was physically abusive. He wouldn't even come back at the boys verbally.

I pleaded with Chad, "Please don't go after your father; he's not worth your getting in trouble over." I was so afraid Chad might lose it one day and do something he would live to regret. He had gone after his father with a bat once. Another time he smashed a lamp over Brad's head. Both times my husband ended up with a deep gash in his head and bled heavily. Once Chad poured a five-gallon can of tar all over Brad's truck.

Both the boys were excellent students. Unfortunately, due to Chad's illness and hospitalization, he was forced to repeat a whole semester in college. This happened twice.

I think that was one of the things that made this situation even more difficult for me. The kids had been through so much and they were such good kids that I wanted to do everything possible to give them some happiness, however brief it may have been.

Already Chad knew he wanted to be an architect. I had managed to get him a drafting table and a lamp that he could clamp on it. I got him all the necessary equipment.

So on February 14, 1989, I entered Circuit City and filled out an application for instant credit. Nothing was in my own name. Usually it took a half hour to be approved. Meanwhile, I went browsing through the aisles as I contemplated which items I would choose.

I had chosen two remote cars, speakers for the stereo, and a VCR.

When an hour had passed, I knew without any doubt this would be my last venture. I was being stalled and hoped it was just paranoia that every eye in the store was on me. For the life of me, I could not think of a way to bolt out of that store. Then, out of the corner of my eye, I saw a man in a police uniform enter the store, and I headed for the ladies' room. Before I reached it, I saw a waste basket and dropped my keys in it.

"Freeze! You're under arrest. Don't take another step!" the officer roared.

HANDCUFFS AND JAIL

After being booked, I was allowed to make one phone call to my son.

"Eric, I've been arrested." I gave him the address of where the car was.

He was not surprised. Both of my sons were just waiting for that phone call. It was not my first arrest. The other times, I had used aliases. With the recent advances in technology, it wouldn't take long before my finger-prints were run through the computer and reveal they all belonged to me.

My first three nights were spent in a crowded hold-ing cell appropriately named the "Tombs." I slept on the cement floor for those three nights. The officers threw the brown paper bags containing bologna sandwiches and milk at us like they were feeding animals in a cage.

I felt like a diver who had surfaced too quickly. One minute I was walking around with total freedom, and the next, I was thrust into a new environment of deprivation.

After my arraignment, I was transferred to Sybil Brand, Los Angeles County's women's jail. I could have almost welcomed this forced vacation had I not had so many concerns about my kids, especially Chad's illness.

After my arrest Eric went back to live with his father and grandmother. Brad seldom came home. He knew what had happened to me, but he didn't care.

All my basic needs were taken care of. I didn't have to go grocery shopping or cook meals. Sleeping, showering, getting dressed, socializing, and crying were all lived out in this same small space day after day, month after month. The only thing changing on a daily basis was the inmates, as the twenty-four-hour revolving door released the old and brought in the new.

I bonded with women I wouldn't even speak to outside of the cement walls. Our conversations were limited to the crimes we were there for. I learned more about drugs and chemical companionship than I cared to know. It amazed me that ninety-nine percent of these girls were not the least bit deterred by their incarceration. They lived and breathed for that moment when they would be released and back on the streets to hit the pipe or get their next fix. The few days they spent in the county jail were nothing more than a minor inconvenience.

I watched women go through seizures and vomiting, and a few days later, they'd be angry at the injustice of having to suffer through this "cold turkey" routine. One woman, who had been there for a while, went to the infirmary every few days where they administered maintenance doses of Methadone. Then I watched her return with this artificial high and just kick back like she was in paradise.

Eric came to see me as often as he could. I will never forget his first visit. I was escorted to the elevator that would take me to the visitors' area. It was a strange experience to step into an elevator with no buttons to push. Everything is electronically controlled and the entire environment hermetically-sealed.

As I got closer to the visitors' area, I felt my composure begin to crack. The mere thought of my sixteen-year-old son visiting me in jail was appalling. I was Suzie Homemaker, Nancy Nurse; I didn't belong here. How did he even find this place that was hidden behind the hills in Los Angeles? In my worst nightmare I could never have thought this day was even remotely possible.

The guard asked, "What's the matter with you?"

I began to answer with a tremble in my voice and then chose not to respond. She wouldn't understand the depth of my shame at facing my son in this place. As I approached the little cubicle with the glass divider and phone, I wanted to crawl into the nearest hole and die. Andre was there with him.

It was a difficult visit. I couldn't stop crying. I was only allowed twenty minutes. I had so much I wanted to say. I had so many questions to ask Eric. They had so many questions to ask me. But I could only talk on the phone to one at a time, and we kept rushing to say all that needed to be said.

Eric was still attending high school along with working nights as a dispatcher for an alarm company. Andre's weekly visits became my lifeline to the outside world. He gave me money to purchase cigarettes, shampoo, and snacks.

I told Chad not to visit. He was feeling somewhat better, and I didn't want the stress of seeing me in jail to cause a flare-up. He did visit me the week of Mother's Day, and it was really good to see him. We had a nice talk, even though it was on a phone with glass between us. He left the guard twenty-five single dollar bills to give me and had written, "I love you, Mom," on each one. I cried all the way back to the dorm.

Chad was also working part time. Between my mother-in-law and the two kids working, they were skimming by financially. My husband did contribute to the rent.

There were times attempting something as simple as making a phone call became a major feat. We had to fight our way through the crowd just to get on the phone within the allotted time.

The lying, the bribing, and the promises rolled off tongues with the ease of the inmates' next breath. There is no such thing as integrity or honor in a county jail.

If you were in the right place at the right time when a detainee was leaving, she would bequeath you a small cardboard box. This was a very exciting ritual. The drawback: knowing as soon as I left for a visit or went to court, some items would be missing when I returned.

As one who had several charges against me, I kept getting transferred from one dorm to another. One week, I was county property; the next week, I was state property. There was no prior warning when this action would take place until the intercom resounded, "Roni Jordan, you're moving. Report immediately to your officer."

The cardboard box that was my bedroom set remained behind, along with my cigarettes, aspirin, shampoo, pencils, and notepaper. It took weeks to accumulate these items, and in one quick heartbeat, they were all gone. This only added to my mounting depression.

The only place to hide from all the noise and the loud voices was in the shower. "We have things to do, places to go, and people to see" is sort of a joke you hear a lot in jail. In truth, we had no place to go, and that gave us the benefit of spending an hour or more in the shower if we so desired. We had nothing but time, and it became both our enemy and our luxury. We spent hours thinking of ways to look presentable for our visitors with the little we had access to. I was still in the county facility and had several court dates before my final sentencing.

It was sad to see so much talent and creativity wasted. Many of the girls wrote beautiful poetry, and several had awesome voices. The artwork I saw could have been displayed in a museum. With the right opportunity to channel their unique skills, most of those girls could have been living very happy, prosperous lives.

We sat for hours unwinding rolls of toilet paper and wadding it up loosely to use as pillows. Toilet paper was also used to make hair rollers; the trick was not getting caught with them in your hair. Using state property for anything other than its intended purpose was illegal.

This small world—with all its noise and chatter—could really test your endurance levels. Simple misunderstandings could escalate into a major fiasco. Interfering in a card game by standing behind a person and revealing what was in her hand, even in a joking manner, or looking at someone the wrong way could cause some tense moments. Most of these women were walking time bombs, and they'd get in your face and cuss you out.

Prison is full of codes of conduct. One of the unwritten rules is that you don't let people run over you; I learned that early on. Any display of gentleness or kindness in that environment was taken as a sign of weakness, and you would be taken advantage of.

I recall one time I had lent a girl some money, and when she returned from a visit with her mother, she lied and told me her mother hadn't given her any money. I lost my temper. I lunged at her and grabbed her shirt, and we really got into it.

She went up to the officer and showed her the scratches I had inflicted, and immediately my name was called over the loudspeaker. "Roni Jordan, report to the front desk."

As I approached and told the guard who I was, she laughed. Forty-seven is certainly not old, but I was considerably older than Karen. The officer could not believe that this twenty-year-old had allowed me to get the upper hand. The officer had two suggestions. To me, "Don't ever lend anyone money." To Karen, "If you can't defend yourself, that's your problem. Don't come to me."

By the end of the fifth month, I still had no clue what my final sentence would be or when it would come. The days dragged on and on. Even now, I'm not sure whether sitting in the dorm all day or being pulled out for another court appearance was the better or worse deal. The degradation of being shackled and handcuffed for hours was horrible, along with the crude invasions called body searches (one more humiliation visited upon the inmate).

One of the more upsetting ordeals was the constant "raids" or "shakedowns". It could be two in the morning or five in the evening when the storm troopers would bust into the dorms or cells and toss everything. Mattresses were thrown against the wall; the bedding was thrown in piles, along with food and personal belongings. What little we had was heartlessly strewn about: letters, court papers, pictures, everyone's belongings were thrown together in heaps. It was like putting a jigsaw puzzle back together after they left.

The loneliness at times was unbearable, and it's the one thing that couldn't be shared. Whoever wrote the following knew what they were talking about: *Loneliness is a cold wind that blows in the corridors of an inmate's life. Sometimes it seems to howl, and at other times, it just whispers, but it never entirely goes away. Its walls echo with only the beating of the inmate's heart.*

Activity makes the time go faster, so you grab any opportunity that will help keep your mind occupied. We'd roll cigarettes or make a paste out of raspberry Kool-Aid to use as hair dye.

I remember one girl carving names out of the little bars of soaps they gave us. Those same little bars of soap are what we used to do our laundry. Grinding it down into little flakes was another way of passing time.

Distractions, such as talking or watching television, are short-lived. Waiting is the name of the game. I'd sit on my bunk for hours during count-time, which is done four times a day. I'd have to wait in line for hours for my medication or to see a doctor. I'd wait in line for hours for my meals. I'd wait in the boarding area to be handcuffed and shackled and then wait my turn to get on the bus. Then the bus would stop at the Los Angeles men's county jail, and I'd have to get off and wait for the men to be processed and shackled. And then I waited for the bus that would take me to whichever court I had to appear at. The men and women drove together for all court appearances. And then the process repeated itself on the return home. On court days, I had to be up at 4 a.m. and didn't return until 7 or 8 p.m. Those days really tested my emotional capacity.

I will never forget the day a judge made a personal remark to a courtroom full of people regarding an offense I had committed in another county. Under no circumstances is a lawyer or judge allowed even to hint at an offense committed in another jurisdiction. I still faced having to appear at some future date in Ventura County for that offense. I was denied the right to speak to my public defender. Appearing in court in state-issued clothes and without benefit of a private attorney can mean the difference between five months and five years.

These events took place many years ago, but for me they will always be yesterday. My body still tenses just thinking of all the sounds. Many of the inmates had been there at least twice before. There are addicts who are desperate and street wise. There are prostitutes who have been used and abused. Of all the sounds I was subjected to, their high pitched screeches still grate on my nerves. As I sit here writing about it, I can *feel* the noise. The voices *vibrate* in my head. Every sound is magnified. Every word uttered echoes inside those cement walls. I can still hear the voices fighting to be heard above all the others. The screaming over who is right or who is the toughest. I just wanted to scream, "Shut up, everyone just shut your mouth." Their rawness and crassness were far from what I was used to. The vulgarity, the shouting, the fighting, and the threats were not just an occasional problem. There is so much anger enclosed within those walls.

The nights were an eternity. One of the oldest prison proverbs is: "Everyone cries at night." I never fell asleep before three o'clock, and it seemed like only seconds before the bugle blew and the steel doors groaned open. If you wanted breakfast, you had one minute to get out before the door snapped shut. It was just time enough to dry the eyes and begin the tedious routine all over again.

As rude and inconsiderate as many of these women were, once I had a chance to talk to them on a one-on-one basis, I saw just how much alike we were.

None of us had clicked our heels like Dorothy in *The Wizard of Oz* and wished to be magically transported to a cell. We were all there for different reasons. Many truly were victims of circumstances, and some didn't even know why they were there. Of course, some wouldn't ever admit to doing anything *illegal*. Others would brag about their conquests.

Twice a day you would hear the officers over the loudspeaker, "Okay, ladies, it's time for your meds. Line up outside the dorm." At least 90% of the girls would make a mad dash to the door so they could be first in line.

I asked a few of the girls, "What meds are you taking?" They all said, "Don't know the name, but it sure calms me down." At that point I asked to see the psychiatrist. Who would have thought my first ever visit to a shrink would be in a jail? He prescribed Sinequan, the tranquilizer of choice for most inmates. We were now into May, and I had been in jail for three months, and for the first time I was able to sleep through the night.

I was hired to work the graveyard shift in the kitchen. This helped to bring about some semblance of normality in this very abnormal environment. I was happy to be in the kitchen working with all the other girls. I had my first banana in three months. We also prepared meals for the officers. So we got to sneak in some real treats. One morning a week the inmates were served pancakes. That was the only morning every girl came to breakfast. My shift started at 11 p.m. Well, I made batter and flipped pancakes for eight solid hours. It was fun, as much as fun can be in that environment. It was cool working along with other girls and talking and fooling around.

The biggest advantage to working the graveyard shift was going back to the dorm and being so tired. And with the tranquilizer I managed to the sleep through the noise and loudspeaker until 6 p.m. Then I went to dinner, and afterwards a few of us just sat around on our bunks talking. Sometimes I would play cards. Before I knew it, it was time to report to the kitchen.

Nothing is quite as simple as it sounds. Reporting to work meant being searched before and after we changed clothes. And before we went on duty and after the shift was over. We were under constant supervision in the kitchen, and those guards really worked us.

I was praying that my next court appearance would be my last.

Unless a person has previous involvement in the penal system, most are unaware of what the following two words mean. The first word is *concurrent* and the second is *consecutive.* Even as a person who has had both words tacked on to my sentence, it's still impossible for me to make sense of them.

It is entirely up to the judge to determine whether your sentence, whatever it may be, will run concurrently or consecutively. In other words, if you have a few offenses and are tried separately for each one and are sentenced to six months for each offense, if the judge says to be served *concurrently,* that means you serve a total of six months. Regardless of the fact that you have committed three different felonies in different places and on three different dates.

But if the judge says six months to run *consecutively,* that means you will serve six months for each of those three offenses. Now you're looking at eighteen months.

The most interesting part of this whole scenario is the fact that most of the inmates can tell you in advance what your sentence will be. They've been through the courts so many times they know exactly how long each sentence is for all the various felonies. They even knew which judges ran sentences concurrently or consecutively. It's mind-boggling.

Believe it or not I had been rearrested while incarcerated. After the alias I had used was run through the system and my fingerprints popped up, it showed I had already been on probation for a previous offense, and another warrant was issued for my arrest. Now for the first time they knew my real name. I lost track of how many times I had to appear in court. The days just run together, and when they called my name at 4 a.m. to tell me I had to be on the bus in forty-five minutes, I just got up. I never had any idea of the date. Eventually, I stopped caring. One day slowly melted in to the next and in to the next. For each offense, I had to appear for arraignment and then something else and something else and then the final sentence was given.

I had already been sentenced to eighteen months for the violation of probation. So my only concern as my final court date approached would be whether the judge would run my sentence concurrently or consecutively.

In June of 1990 I appeared for the last time. Before I went into the courtroom, my public defender told me what the prosecutor was offering, which was six months. It didn't sound all that bad. I just had to pray the judge would say the only word that mattered: concurrently.

I was shocked to hear the word *consecutively* followed by, "Two years to be served in a state penitentiary." Then the gavel descended.

I had been given an additional six months because of the judge's biased opinion about the offense in Ventura County. That was so wrong. I still faced extradition to appear in court there at some point. Everything from here on became covert. I was not given any time frame as to when I would be transferred.

I recalled the morning I woke up and saw the empty bed next to mine. I had befriended the girl who occupied it, and we had been up chatting till midnight. Six hours later she was gone, along with all her bedding. It was eerie. I remember thinking something bad had happened to her. Later that day, I found a note she had left in *my cardboard box* explaining she was being transferred and had not been told in advance.

Three weeks later, the last week of June, that same moment arrived for me. We were awakened one by one at three in the morning and told to take our bedding and report to the front desk. We were warned that all movement was to be done in complete silence, absolutely no talking. I would have to leave all my worldly possessions behind.

Six hours later, we were sitting on a bus shackled and cuffed alongside uniformed escorts, being transported via shotgun to the California Institution for Women in Chino. Breathing was the only activity allowed on the bus. There is no word in any dictionary or thesaurus that could adequately describe the fear and the tension each of us felt. It was beyond frightening. As we drove through the gates, the sign read, "Warning: No Warning Shots Fired!"

Isolation and loneliness became my steady companions.

SHACKLES AND PRISON

California Institution for Women is the largest women's prison in the United States, situated in the middle of the desert and surrounded by cow pastures. It had to be 115 degrees the day we arrived. Between the smell and the heat, I thought surely I had been sent to Calcutta. Twelve hours later, the processing procedure completed, I was personally escorted to a cell that was occupied by a young Asian girl. She was thrilled to have someone to talk to. The first thing I noticed was a newspaper.

"They actually give you a newspaper!" I said.

Chuckling, she replied, "Oh, no, that one has been here for months. That's our fly swatter."

I soon learned killing flies was a full-time job. There was no glass in the window or screen, just bars. Often our wake-up calls came in the form of guards walking along the outside with sledgehammers at five in the morning banging on the bars making sure they were intact.

I had not yet reached the actual prison grounds. I was housed in a separate area and would remain there for six weeks, during which time they do a complete check on all used aliases, FBI check, and outstanding warrants. It's just part of the process.

I immediately requested a visitor form and sent it to Andre. That's another long process because every visitor had to be approved. Doing background checks on visitors could take as long as a month.

This particular building was in the shape of an octagon, and it was one level with all the interior walls of the cells facing an empty courtyard. The yard was about a quarter of a mile in length and width. The second two weeks were kind of fun. We'd all gather at dusk by our barred windows. My cell partner and I and all the girls from the other cells would shout jokes or tell stories across the courtyard. Most of us couldn't see one another or the cells on either side of us, but just the camaraderie of laughing under the stars made it enjoyable. Every night we did this. Of course, it stopped abruptly at 9 p.m. for the count.

It was in this same facility that they had built "The Deep Six" twenty-one years prior. It was a special area constructed for the Manson girls. We never actually passed by it, but on our way to meals, we could look down that long corridor and we'd get that creepy feeling knowing we were close to an area we had heard so much about. The inmates had all heard the stories about Charles Manson and his girls but were too young to have been affected by the brutality of all those murders.

My third week there, I was moved to a dorm, which was cool; there were about twenty-five women in this area. It was strange to have been there three weeks, and in all that time, I had not had access to a mirror. But we grew to see ourselves in others.

The only activities were playing Monopoly or cards. If you weren't doing either of those, you stayed on your bunk. Sitting on someone else's bunk was taboo.

The meals were far better than the county jail slop. For us new arrivals, we thought they had made a mistake and had brought us to a restaurant when we saw the salad next to our plates. A few days later, I sat down at the table and ate the most delicious steak I had ever had.

"Wow, that steak was great," I said.

"Ha, that wasn't steak. That was liver."

I thought I was going to be sick. You know you've been in too long when something you detest melts on your palate as if it's a gourmet meal.

Six weeks later, after the state completed its full investigation, my background check was finished, and they knew I had no gang affiliations, I was released from my temporary housing in the dorm along with about ten other women. We now took the long walk across the entire prison yard and entered the big house. Here, I met up with several girls from Los Angeles County. Reunion time! This was as close to home as it was going to get for a long time.

I was out of the octagon-shaped building and into what truly looked like a prison you see on television. I was back in a 9' x 4' cell with solid steel doors that had to be opened by a central control station. There were no bars. The only thing in the middle top section of the door was a 10" x 10" wicket, which is similar to a ticket office with grating.

After putting all my belongings in the cell, I went to lunch, and then I was allowed outside for two hours.

It felt like heaven to have the freedom to be outdoors for a while. It happened to be a Sunday, and at six o'clock, they were holding a service in the chapel.

I will never forget those first twenty minutes in the chapel.

"You see that girl sitting in front of you?" Betty asked.

"Yes," I said.

"That's Susan Atkins!"

There I sat, inches away from a woman who had committed the most heinous crimes ever recorded and a person I had loathed for years.

Those murders were committed three weeks before my son Chad was born. What she did to actress Sharon Tate and her unborn child was diabolical. I ran out of the chapel.

The realization of where I had come from and where I was at that moment left me depressed for days.

There was another time Susan Atkins sat at the table with me for lunch. I couldn't keep myself from staring at this slim thirty-seven-year-old woman with salt and pepper hair pulled up in a ponytail. She looked like she belonged in a *Happy Days* sitcom. She ate her meals with a spoon just like the rest of us. She got up and went to work like the rest of the inmates. She had to be the vilest woman in that prison, yet she had a mother somewhere.

Pasquale once said, "We are all capable of the sewer and the palace." In a police lineup, most inmates would be indistinguishable from Sunday school teachers.

I learned a tough lesson my first week.

"How long are you in for?" I asked a girl I was having lunch with.

"I'm a lifer!" she responded. "A word of warning, don't ever ask anyone that question again."

It was good advice, because just hearing that word *lifer* left me stunned. I could not imagine spending the rest of my days in that environment.

I would lie in my bunk at night wondering what it would be like knowing I would never leave the grounds of that prison. I would never taste a hot fudge sundae, go bowling, or see a Broadway show. There were rumors that Ms. Atkins had her cell carpeted and a few additional amenities. But whatever they were, and no matter how many comforts the cell had, it was still a tiny hollow cell with bars and a lock.

I can recall having breakfast with a young, very pretty girl. I knew from the prison gossip she was serving thirty-two years for kidnapping. There were women in there for sexual crimes on kids, murderers, and they all looked like the girl next door.

It was a culture of absolute dependency. You couldn't just hop off your bunk and walk to the restroom when you needed to go. You had to ask and be given permission. If it was during count time, you learned to wait. The counts were done four times a day. All activity would come to an abrupt halt, and we had to remain seated on our bunks while the guards went around the dorms and all the cells to check each individual wristband. This took a minimum of an hour, and it's quite a fascinating ritual knowing that every county jail, along with every state and federal prison in California, was doing this in tandem. If the count was incorrect, it meant sitting on your bunk for hours until it was exact. There were a few times we didn't get dinner until nine or ten o'clock in the evening or not at all.

As soon as I had phone privileges I called Eric and Chad. I was elated that they were home. It was so good to talk to them. I had already written to them so they knew where I was. They, in turn, called Andre for me and told him I would be moving out of CIW within a few days. I was thrilled the next day when one of the guards approached me and told me I had a visitor. This was sometime in the middle of August and would be my first contact visit with anyone since my arrest.

During this time, my mother had written me and enclosed the invitation to my thirtieth class reunion. It was a year away and had been sent to my parents' home. I was bewildered trying to comprehend her reasoning for sending it to me. It was not something I cared to think about. It hurt. I could still recall the caption beneath my yearbook picture, "Future Homemaker of America." Yeah, that was me, now sitting in my state-issued clothes with "Inmate" stenciled across the back and eating in a "chow hall," three thousand miles away.

I've been asked numerous times if prison was anything like you see in the movies. One thing made my incarceration different. First, there has never been a movie made about women housed in a men's prison. Secondly, I was forty-seven years old and forced to play the part of the street-wise convict. I was anything but street-wise, but I learned quickly.

Prison life is as different from county jail as the cheap motel is different from the Waldorf Astoria. The influx of detainees in the county jails is like something you'd see on an assembly line that runs twenty-four-seven. By the time you reach the penitentiary, you've already had months to prepare for the serious business that lies ahead. Prison avails you a more normal way of life and the atmosphere a higher caliber. It is a no-nonsense environment. CIW reminded me very much of a college campus except for the chain link fences, the tightly coiled razor-sharp wire, and the stark reality that envelops your very being when you look up and see the guards in the tower walking around the perimeter carrying rifles and shotguns, knowing your fate is in their hands.

It's prison as we know prison to be, where the nature of the life within is predatory, the weak will be preyed upon, and the guards will abuse their authority. At the slightest sign of an altercation on the grounds, we drop immediately when the whistle blows and those guards roll up to the scene.

There were times I happened upon some women fighting, and it was something I was tempted to stand around and watch. It passed the time. But I didn't want to be too close, because they would round everyone up. Even people who had nothing to do with the disturbance could spend days, even weeks, in lockup.

I remember having to attend orientation classes the first five days we moved over to the big yard. Those lectures left us with no doubt that we were in the *big house.* The thing that I found most frightening was being told that snitches were not tolerated in this environment. And a week later, when my cell-partner came back from a visit with a stash of pot, I feared for my life. I had never smoked pot and certainly wouldn't try it at this point.

On the flip-side, it had its benefits, as long we didn't get caught. We had a little convenience store going on. It was great. She traded for cigarettes and all kinds of goodies. And she shared everything with me. The problem was, if they found the pot in our cell, I would be going down with her.

The officers didn't care how it got in there or who it belonged to, we would both be hauled out and taken back to Los Angeles and back into court with more time added to our present sentences.

CIW was in the process of changing into a prison that housed inmates doing life sentences, long-term sentences, or for women with AIDS, which meant several of us had to be transferred to Avenal State Prison for Men. Yes, I did say *men*. I was one of the chosen because they found an outstanding warrant on me in Ventura County. I would have to be extradited there to appear in court.

Another covert transport took place sometime during the first week of August. I was shackled and handcuffed once again, and twelve hours later, delivered to Avenal, California's finest men's prison out in the middle of no-man's land. It had eight yards, each one housing three units, which looked like humongous cement silos. Three of the yards were presently housing the women. Each yard was self-contained, surrounded by a high, barbed-wire fence about a mile apart from one another. The entire acreage of Avenal was the size of a small city.

In the evening, we had free time for an hour. Half of the inmates are wannabes, and they would work out, lift weights, and do bench presses for hours. After a few months, they really did look like guys. They'd get the zigzag buzz cuts and the bandanas. The muscles were pumped up. I would play spades every night with these girls, and if you were to take a quick glance our way, you'd swear I was playing with a bunch of guys.

I never encountered any problems with these girls. We all have an aura about us, and when you live in these confined quarters, the waves go out with the proper signals. These girls know immediately which ones are looking to mess around, and they know which ones aren't. I talked so much about my kids and Andre, it became a signal, and they knew immediately to stay away.

The interesting thing was that what my felonies consisted of really put me on a higher level. Not that I ever saw myself as better than any of them. I really didn't. Even the judge had, on more than one occasion, referred to me as a sophisticated white-collar criminal. I wasn't there for using or selling drugs or prostitution. My offenses were all very serious. They included grand theft auto, grand theft, bank robbery, forgery, absconding, prescription forgery, and violation of probation. But no weapons were ever involved. No one had ever been assaulted or harmed due to my actions.

Avenal was hardcore and definitely not a place for the shy or timid. We were completely stripped of any dignity. There was no privacy. Even the toilets were out in the open and, yes, in full view of every inmate and guard. Most of the officers were male. There were no individual showers or curtains, just one big area exposed to the watchful eyes of all who had sight.

Running the track became routine; when boredom set in, we ran backward. It was hot there, so hot you could see the heat mirages floating before your eyes. Sometimes we'd see little dust devils (whirlwinds) of sagebrush and tumbleweed spinning around. You remember these things because you welcomed any diversion that helped pass the time.

I remember lying awake at night wondering how many thousands of men had passed through the gates here. How many murderers, armed robbers, drug smugglers, rapists, or even worse, had slept in this same bunk I was now in? How many secrets did those concrete walls hold? How many screams had they heard? *Déjà vu!*

I had experienced this same startling and frightening feeling once before at CIW. That precise moment, I could see the gravity of what I had done to bring me to this place. It was a place every human being lives in fear of, a place you drive by and shudder just thinking of the people on the other side. It's the only place you pray never to see the inside of.

Yet *cop* shows keep many people glued to the television. The intrigue and mystique of what it's like on the inside captures and captivates the mind of those who have never been there. They definitely don't want any part of it, but voyeurism in this situation is okay.

For me personally, I love watching *Law and Order, CSI Miami, Las Vegas,* and *New York.* This part of my life took place so many years ago that I still find it hard to comprehend that I actually was part of many scenes in these shows. What I like most is to compare what I see on these shows to what I know really takes place.

Two months later, in the beginning of October, without warning, I was extradited to Ventura County, which is quite a process. There were four women, including myself, from various facilities being transported in a regular van, no visible signs to alert passing vehicles that we were "those bad people."

The guards stayed in constant radio contact with officers driving ahead. Every few miles, the van stopped at checkpoints, and the guards got out, making sure nothing was out of the ordinary or that any decoys were preparing to intercept the van. It's exactly the same as when heads of state or the president are being escorted somewhere. To be a part of something that looks so Hollywood but was truly happening to me and was so dangerous was surreal.

My heart was throbbing in the excitement of the moment, along with the fear that if I made one wrong move either a bullet would be penetrating my skull or piercing my chest. Maybe not a move I might make, but even a move made by a scurrying chipmunk could bring an end to my life.

I felt much safer being transported on the bus. The officers assigned to transport us were not secret service agents riding shotgun to protect me. They were there to protect society *from* me, and there wouldn't be a moment's hesitation to aim and fire.

I was put in another new environment for three months. This time, it was multi-tiered cell blocks.

The individual cells were exactly the same as CIW. They all had the solid steel doors controlled by a central station. There were about six cells to each pod. I have no idea what pod stands for, but all the sections were referred to as pods. I was allowed out of the cell a few times a day. There was one big room one level below, and there were four stainless steel tables cemented into the floor. All our meals were delivered to this area. There was one television. The only program I can recall everyone agreeing on was *The Simpsons*.

Twelve women were housed in this area, bringing the noise level down ten notches. Whenever I left the cell I would go down to play cards. Every jail has a few decks of cards.

The one good thing about being in Ventura County jail was Andre's weekly visits. Things were moving too fast, and it would probably be another six months before he would have been approved for visits at Avenal. Here in the county jail, he was allowed to visit without prior approval.

The court routine started again, only this time I didn't have to get on a bus. We walked through the underground tunnel. I nicknamed it the *Tunnel of Tears,* because it was a place that had seen and heard many cries.

I will never forget the first week I was there and saw the girls washing their clothes in the toilets and hanging them up to air dry. Around midnight, they would fold them in a particular fashion so they would have creases, and then they'd tuck them under the one-inch mattress and sleep on them. I'm not kidding; by morning they looked like they had just come from the dry cleaners. It was a necessary inconvenience if you were scheduled to be in court and wanted to look presentable. We were only issued one set of clothes weekly. I fell in line, and within a few weeks I was also washing my clothes in the bowl. Survival of the fittest!

Here's another example of how clever some of these girls are. I was amazed the first time my cellmate emptied the toilet bowl. I forget exactly how it was done. But at a predetermined time with a few other girls, Ellen would empty the bowl, and we could shout to one another through the bowl. Obviously it was just something to keep us occupied and pass the time. There was no real need to converse with our fellow inmates since we spent time together at meals and free time. It sounded very hollow, like we were shouting from a cave. I sometimes wonder if that's how the term cell phone came into existence.

The week before Thanksgiving I appeared in court for the last time. The judge sentenced me to a year to run *consecutively*. I wanted to scream, "But Judge, I'm already doing time for that offense!"

I was still there at Thanksgiving to experience another flashback moment during our special dinner.

"How come this chicken is so tough?" I asked a girl sitting at the table with me.

"That's not chicken; that's rabbit," she said with a crude snicker.

"Oh no, please don't tell me it's one of those I see lying on the side of the freeway!"

For dessert, we were given two chocolate cupcakes. Let the pilgrims have their pumpkin pie; I savored those cupcakes for the entire evening, making the rabbit a distant memory.

The first week in December I was transported back to Avenal. This meant no more little cartons of milk with our meals. Now we were back to Avenal's infamous "Jim Jones Punch", which was vile and served at every meal.

Arriving back for a second time was far more depressing than the first time I arrived. Before I had left Avenal I had accumulated a fair amount of items. Andre sent money and with that I was able to buy cigarettes, candy, and a lot of personal items. I wasn't allowed to take any of it to Ventura and upon returning everything was gone. Believe me they don't keep anything stored for you.

The weather had turned cold. The surrounding desert at Avenal represented a far greater menace than the prison itself. There was not a blade of grass or a tree anywhere. As far as the eye could see, there was nothing but dirt and mountains. I wouldn't have known the difference if they had blindfolded me and dropped me in the Sahara. It was a desolate and depressing setting both inside and outside the razor-sharp fences.

By the middle of the month I was working as a porter, which meant cleaning this huge place that housed about 150 women. Three of us mopped the concrete floors and scoured the bathrooms every morning, noon, and night. These were not enclosed showers or toilets with doors. This was a men's prison, and privacy had not been even a thought when Avenal had been built.

Every Thursday there was an official inspection. And I am by no means exaggerating when I say this inspection was as thorough as any inspection in a marine barracks. Every bunk had to be scrubbed with disinfectant. The mattress was removed, and every nook and cranny of the metal frame was scrubbed and every coil and spring was scrubbed too. The inside of the building was all cinder block. And yes, we had to scrub every block around all the bunk areas. The sinks and toilets had to sparkle. The showers had to be spic and span. All the stainless steel tables had to shine.

We had a choice of staying inside and cleaning for four hours. Or we could choose to remain outside. But whatever choice we made, that was engraved in stone. Once we were outside we couldn't even go inside to use the bathroom. We sat outside in the bitter cold and did nothing for those four hours. I sometimes stayed in to clean, and other times I remained outside. To this day I honestly don't know which was preferable. A whole bunch of us would sit on the bleachers and yak away for four hours, which seemed like an eternity. We had no gloves. But most of us had cigarettes.

Shortly after lunch, the sergeant and his entourage would appear. They would go over every inch of that building, and believe it or not, the sergeant wore a while glove to check for dust.

There were no demerits or punishment if we didn't pass. However, we were graded on how clean our building was. This was a huge competition, because if our building came in first, we went to the chow hall first. Being second wasn't too bad. But you never wanted to be third because nine out of ten times there was very little food left. And this process continued for a whole week. The worst part about being at the bottom was having to return and listen to all the other girls brag about what a great dinner they had and about the apple pie they enjoyed. Meanwhile, we didn't have a hamburger or apple pie. But they always had plenty of the Jim Jones punch.

For me, the worst part was having to wait our turn. The winners got to dinner at five thirty. The runner-ups went at six thirty. And the losers had to wait until they returned and didn't get to eat until seven thirty or eight o'clock in the evening. And added to that was the bitter cold and having to walk a very long distance to the chow hall. Then returning very late and in the dark.

Of course, these rules also applied to breakfast and lunch.

The "Med Call" followed immediately after meals. And again, if you were in the third group, there was no way you could reach the infirmary area in time to get your meds. And there was absolutely no running allowed on the grounds.

Christmas was approaching, and its nearness added to my ever-mounting depression.

Every other day the mail was delivered, and we'd sit on our bunks while the guards called to those who had mail. Another reason for depression amongst inmates. It was hard to sit there and listen to the same names being called every time, and often one person would get a whole bunch of letters and others got none. I got a few. Andre wrote regularly. I can't tell you how important mail is to an inmate.

One of those times I was sitting on my bunk as the mail was being dispersed, and when they were done, one of the guards roared.

"Stay on your bunks."

To this day, if I close my eyes, I can still see the officers tossing us bags of shelled peanuts like we were animals in a cage!

"Merry Christmas!" they shouted.

Now to heap insult upon insult, the prison was running low on toilet paper. It didn't seem like a big deal in the beginning, but two weeks later they were rationing the toilet paper. Before you know it, we were each given a roll of paper, and we had to keep it in our locker and remember to bring it with us every time we went to the "toilet on exhibition." Talk about chaos.

Sure, we all had our own individual lockers, but there were no locks. Need I say more?

We spent New Year's Eve in lockdown. We had to remain on our bunks for the entire evening. No television. No playing cards. We were told that there had been a murder attempt in one the buildings that housed the men. We never did find out the details or whether anyone had died. It was a very creepy feeling.

Sometime during the first week in January 1991, there was a flood in our building, and I slipped while mopping the floor. I had to wait until four o'clock the following morning, limp a quarter of a mile to the infirmary, and then stand outside in the bitter cold waiting my turn to see a doctor. The line was a mile long every morning, and it was freezing. Happy New Year!

That same week, the pipes froze, leaving us without heat for five days. To combat the freezing temperatures, the state issued each of us an army blanket. We were also without hot water for that same length of time. Hundreds of girls left at four o'clock in the morning to be driven out to the abattoir where they slaughtered chickens all day or worked in the pig pens only to return twelve hours later to jump into a freezing cold shower.

This was a men's prison, and there was no job distinction. Working is of the utmost of importance, because it's the only way to get your sentencing time reduced. Good behavior is another incentive to get even more time deducted. Good time and work time are catch phrases among inmates. You will do whatever is necessary to get an early release, including feeding pigs, killing chickens, or cleaning bathrooms.

The second week in January, I was upgraded and started working in the sergeant's office. I had to type statements against inmates caught in lesbian activity. Needless to say, it was more than a full-time job.

Fortunately, there were tons of books floating around. There was also a small library. Reading became my salvation, and I welcomed every opportunity to get lost for a few hours in those pages.

On February 6, 1991, I was released. This came well in advance of the date I originally was scheduled for release. Between the work time and good behavior, my sentence was cut in half. I was shocked when I heard my name called over the loudspeaker to report to the sergeant's office whereupon he asked me, "How would you like to go home?" I honestly thought he was joking. Years later I would think back and be so grateful. I had been released from prison as dramatically as St. Paul, when an angel of the Lord freed him from his prison cell.

I was driven by one of the corrections officers to the train station. He purchased a one-way ticket to Van Nuys for $39 and gave me the balance of my gate money.

I took a cab from the train station to the apartment. Eric arrived home at ten o'clock wearing a knee brace. At three o'clock in the morning, just six hours after I arrived home, my husband walked in drunk. Nothing had changed.

The following morning, I reported to the parole office. The provisions of my parole mandated I live with my family for one year. And since that included living with my husband, I was ordered to attend Al-anon meetings and codependency meetings weekly. Lastly, I was to find a job immediately. And I could not, under any circumstances, lie on any job application.

RETURN TO SOCIETY

While I was in prison, Eric had the use of my car. He was active in the Key Club and was dating a girl he had met there. Both were good kids and excellent students. Chad was in his second year of college and doing very well.

That was only on the surface, however. Chad and Eric have always been very different, and from all outward appearances, I believe Eric accepted the circumstances. But Chad was full of anger, and there were more than a few times he physically went after his father.

I have never asked him directly what his feelings are. I didn't want him to lie to me, nor did I want him to tell me the truth. I do know he had lived in fear of me getting arrested and blamed his father for my being forced to steal. There was one absolute: My love for my sons would compel me to do whatever was necessary to feed them and care for them. I would never, ever abandon them willingly.

During my incarceration, I wrote to my parents but never disclosed what I had done. How could I expect them, at the age of seventy, to understand the complexity of my situation? My mother wrote back, and we continued to correspond.

There was no more criticism. I knew she was truly concerned, but her concern was directed more to my sons. Chad and Eric had both visited my parents during the summer while I was incarcerated. For the first time my mother respected me enough to write and ask me if they could visit. I had no problem with that. It had never been my intention to keep the boys from seeing their grandparents. And they were old enough now that she couldn't keep them there against their will.

I was elated that both of them wanted to see their grandparents. Grandparents are grandparents, and every kid knows the importance of having them.

My father's mother was the only grandparent I knew, and she passed away when I was seven. My kids were very lucky to have all four grandparents for a good many years.

Chad and his friend Josh took a road trip across country. They stayed with my parents for a few days.

Eric was offered an opportunity to take part in a summer program at a college on the east coast. My parents paid his tuition, and they also paid for his trip back to visit with them before he began classes.

Two months after my release, in April, Chad's illness flared up, causing him excruciating pain and profuse bleeding. The remission period had ended. Without medical insurance, he had to be admitted to a county hospital, and this time, I could do nothing to get money to help him.

For three weeks, they did every possible test and procedure, hoping for a sudden miracle; but when the bleeding and the pain worsened, we had to face the inevitable. He was scheduled to undergo one of the most radical surgeries I know of, removal of his entire large colon. He would then have an ileostomy bag attached to his abdomen. There was no coming to terms with any of this. I wondered why, at the age of twenty, my son had to suffer this indignity.

A month after he entered the hospital, in May, he was prepped and wheeled to the operating room.

As I sat in the waiting room, I recalled ten years prior being scrubbed in on a case in which the surgeon was doing the same operation Chad was now undergoing. In all the years I worked alongside this doctor, I had never seen him lose his temper; but just as we were lifting the colon out of the abdomen, he started cursing and throwing instruments. I don't recall his exact words, but clearly, he felt this operation was preventable.

Evidently, the girl, who was about sixteen, was under a lot of stress because of problems at home and with her parents, but mostly because they had waited so long to seek medical treatment. He was in a rage over the flagrant violation of this young girl's body. She would be left with an ileostomy bag attached to her abdomen for the rest of her life.

I was struck with that thought; was the surgeon who was operating on Chad at this very moment doing the same thing as he lifted out his colon? The brutality of that surgery on my son would visit my dreams and torment me for years.

Twelve hours later, he was taken to the recovery room. Unable to breathe on his own, he remained there for several hours. Then he was taken to the intensive-care unit, where Eric and his girlfriend, Kim, and I had been waiting. I couldn't catch my breath as I was so shocked by his appearance. He looked exactly like one of those helium balloons completely inflated. I know from my own experience working in the operating room this is not uncommon. Because of the length of time he was undergoing surgery and the trauma of it, it causes the tissues to fill up with fluid. He was white as a ghost from losing so much blood. Watching a child suffer is the closest thing to being in hell a parent can ever come. I would have done anything in this world to take on the suffering for him.

Every day, I'd sit in that hospital room and stare at Chad. I wanted to cry and never stop. I must have revisited every nuance from the past five years as I prayed to escape the torrent of guilt that threatened to swallow me. I just kept going over in my head all that he had been through. Certainly the physical trauma and pain was the worst. But every day I'd ask myself how much of this could have been avoided if I'd gotten him to a doctor sooner. I know stress causes colitis in many cases, and he had certainly been through far more stress than most kids. He once told me how many pencil tips he almost chewed off while he was in class because of the pain and the need to go the bathroom and having to hold it.

Ten days later, I was able to bring him home.

The third week in June Eric graduated from high school. How can I describe the emotions of seeing my two sons standing before me? Chad was still very weak but alive and thrilled to be attending his brother's grad-uation. Eric was in his cap and gown graduating with all A's and one B, with teachers' comments: "Excellent student." "Work is outstanding." "A pleasure to have in class."

Admiration seemed like such a trite word. I certainly was not proud of what I had done, but watching them gave me some peace. At least we were still together. No foster homes.

The very next day, Chad was rushed back to the hospital by ambulance with a bowel obstruction. He could barely breathe because the pain was so excruciating. He was discharged seven days later, but he continued to have problems with the ileostomy.

I had to rush him back to the hospital a few times so the doctor could resuture the bag onto his abdomen. When that failed to work, the doctor decided to go ahead and do the second part of the surgery. It was only six weeks since the first operation, and normally they wait a few months, but because of the recurring infections and bleeding around the site, he decided it was necessary to go ahead with it at this time. The bag was removed, and the pull-through procedure was successfully completed. He recovered from that very slowly. His life would never be as normal as other kids his age, but he was alive and well.

Sometime during the later part of October, I started working for an answering service, and life started to imitate what I thought was normal. Chad was feeling much better. Weekends I spent with Andre. Eric still had the use of my car to go to his classes and job. Fortunately I could walk to work. It was only a mile from our apartment.

Chad and I flew back east the following year, in June 1992, to visit my family. It was an emotional and tearful reunion. It was the first time I had seen my niece Ashley.

I had seen my nephews, Jason and Drew, twice when they were infants.

There was no mention of my incarceration or what had transpired five years prior. We had a wonderful two weeks. I did not detect any hint of bitterness or animosity.

I remained in contact with my mother almost weekly, and Dennis called regularly.

The following year I was released from parole and no longer had to live with the family. So in October of 1993, with Andre's help, I moved into my own apartment. There was no doubt that we cared very much for one another. Our biggest disagreements were over my newest problem, which was drinking.

So much had happened that first year after my release. Chad's illnesses and surgeries. Eric moved into the school dorms. He and Kim continued to see one another. Their relationship was getting serious. And Chad returned to college to repeat the two semesters he was out ill. He was also seeing a girl by the name of Dana.

I was still working at the answering service, which was boring. I didn't have a car. I had been living with so much chaos for so many years that settling down into a quiet routine was a challenge. In so many ways my life was much better than ever. But I had missed so many good times and so many years with my sons. They were completely on their own.

I was finding it hard to adjust to life on the outside. It's like living in France for a year, and then when you return to the United States, you can't ever tell anyone that you were in France. I lived with a guard over my mouth, monitoring every word that I spoke. I was so afraid of slipping at work and losing the job. The only way I could find any release was to have a few drinks.

I had never even been a social drinker. Now I was finding the joy of letting go of my inhibitions, and it was wonderful. For a few hours I didn't feel anything, and I could actually forget about the past for a short time. There were periods of elation, and I was glad the boys had their girlfriends and both were doing well in school. And then there were periods when the elation left and reality set back in. Ten years of my life were gone. I began buying a bottle of whiskey to have at home. What the heck, if I was alone I'd have one or two drinks, and then I could forget everything and fall asleep.

The holidays were good. Kim's family was wonderful to Eric and included me in everything. They even had a birthday party for him, and I was invited. I was invited to her aunt's for Thanksgiving. And Christmas Eve they had a big celebration. She had a big family. As much as I enjoyed it, I still had to watch every word out of my mouth for fear of slipping. Christmas morning we went to her mom's for brunch. Everyone bought me presents, but I didn't have any money to reciprocate.

We spent a good part of Christmas Day with Irene. Of course Brad wasn't around. I really felt sorry for my mother-in-law. She was so good-hearted, and she was working so hard. But she never complained.

My drinking continued but not yet to the point I needed a drink every day.

One month later, on January 17, 1994, I woke to violent thrashing. It was like someone had picked up the apartment building and was playing volleyball with it. There were chunks of the ceiling falling on me, and the windows were exploding. Those forty-five seconds turned into what seemed like an eternity. Just as it started to subside and I attempted to get out, it started all over again. I was wedged in the doorframe holding on for dear life. I had no doubt this was the big one, the earthquake that would surely bury California in the ocean.

"Is anyone in there?" some man was shouting. "Get out. The building is collapsing!"

It was 4:30 in the morning and pitch black. I had to claw through the rubble and climb through the shattered window frame, where I landed on shards of broken glass in my bare feet. I ran to the apartment where my mother-in-law and Chad were and screamed for them to get out.

There was a huge explosion three blocks away, where the underground gas line intersected with a gas station. It looked like a war zone. Everyone was in shock. The water line burst and erupted into major flooding on the main street. That hour seemed endless before the first light of day appeared, and we were able to see the devastation.

Two hours later, Eric and Kim arrived. Their apartment had a lot of damage, but the building was still standing.

"Eric, would you and Kim drive me to work?" I asked. "The computers can run on the generators."

"Sure!" he said.

For the next seven days, I worked almost round the clock. I stayed with Eric and Kim for two weeks.

Four of the major freeways had collapsed. One train had derailed. The fires continued to burn.

This was the fifth time I had lost an apartment and all my belongings. I was tired, depressed, and broke. The car that I had just purchased was damaged and no longer running.

At this point, my drinking had escalated to an around-the-clock need. I lived in constant fear of another earthquake. So this became a good reason for me to drink more.

I received a check from FEMA for $2,400. My parents sent me $500, and my brother Todd also sent me $500. I don't know where I would have been without their help. But having to find another apartment, pay the deposit, and buy a car quickly depleted these funds.

I had to completely refurnish the entire apartment, which was really a studio. Every utensil had to be replaced. Andre also helped me on a monthly basis.

By the end of the year, we had experienced more than eight thousand aftershocks from the earthquake, and alcohol had really taken control of me. I could not get through a few hours without a drink, even during the day.

FROM THE GRAVE TO GRACE

I began to drink during work hours. The thing that had really pushed me over the edge was having to work the second shift on December 31. It was New Year's Eve, and I had to work from 7 p.m. until midnight. Andre and I couldn't make any plans.

That night I just couldn't force myself to get ready for work. I was so overcome with depression, I just snapped. In less than five minutes, I downed a quart of whiskey while ingesting a bottle of tranquilizers.

New Year's Day, I went into cardiac arrest. I don't recall a thing until several days later when I heard Chad talking to me. I remained on a respirator for ten days. Once I was stabilized, they transferred me to a trauma center. A month later, I was released.

God was now the wrath of my anger. Why would he bring me back only to face the pain and suffering all over again? I still had pneumonia and was on IV treatments at home. As the fluids dripped into my left arm, I was pouring a glass of whiskey with my right hand.

By March, I sank to an all-time low when I was left with no choice but to take a job in telemarketing. I was no salesperson, and I hated the idea of making cold calls to people and trying to get them to buy computer cartridges. I had worked at the answering service for a few years. I had no problem talking to people on the phone. But there was something about telemarketing that just rubbed me the wrong way. At lunchtime, I would go home and have a few drinks. When I returned, my selling inhibitions disappeared.

Chad had moved to L.A. and was attending architectural college. He was busy with school and work. Eric had graduated from college in June 1995. He and Kim were married in July, and a week later, they moved to D.C., where he would be starting law school at Georgetown University.

I was thrilled about all his accomplishments. I certainly admired his determination to make something of himself. He was really and truly on his own, and that was hard for me to accept. He had a wife and was going to this Ivy League college, and I hadn't been part of any of it.

One day I was rushing off to rescue him from my parents, and now he had a wife and a great future that I would never fit into.

It didn't take long for my coworkers to recognize the obvious signs that I was drinking. Unbeknownst to me, all of the women working there were recovering addicts and alcoholics and were living in the same recovery home.

Within a month, I received a notice that my car was going to be repossessed. The sheriff's department had already been to my apartment personally to hand me my eviction papers.

"Roni, I love you very much," Andre said. "But I can't take your drinking anymore." He moved all my belongings into a storage unit. I had twelve hours left before I had to vacate the premises.

In desperation, I called Chad's girlfriend.

"Dana, it's Roni," I said. "Do you mind if I stay with you for a few days?"

"Sure, for a few days," she said.

A few days turned into two weeks, at which point Dana told me I had to be out by the following Monday. Even she was fed up with my drinking.

That evening, I went to an AA meeting at the recovery home with my coworkers.

I was so happy to be among these girls that I had been working alongside of for two months. It made me feel good to know that they cared enough to invite me there.

I had no clue whatsoever that when I took this job there were girls working there with addiction problems. By the second week they started to recognize that I had a problem. They invited me to join them for lunch.

Try to picture this extraordinary scene.

They put all the chairs in a circle, and we began eating lunch. Suddenly, out of the blue I heard someone say:

"Hi, my name is Karen, and I'm an alcoholic and a drug addict."

If I live to be a hundred I will never forget that girl's name or those words. I was shocked. Why would anyone sit there in front of ten other women and admit to something like that? I thought she had to be nuts. And just then another girl started speaking. I will never forget her name either.

"My name is Catherine, and I am a drug addict and alcoholic."

And this continued through the remaining eight women. At the end of the lunch break, I was convinced they were all nuts. Number one, I had never been to an AA meeting. I had heard the term Alcoholics Anonymous a few times, but I never dreamed this is how they introduced themselves. And I certainly couldn't understand why they invited me to join their inner circle.

I never knew until much later they did that for my sake. The lunch was not an AA meeting. That was for my benefit and to give me some insight into other women who were dealing with a problem I had yet to confront or even acknowledge.

When I went to the meeting at their residency that Wednesday evening, I was at the end of my rope and again questioning why God had kept me alive. I was feeling far worse than I had felt on New Year's Eve. Things had clearly worsened. I had lost the job at the answering service. I hated this telemarketing business. I don't know what I would have done if my car had been repossessed. I was homeless. Once again what little I owned was in storage. I was making next to nothing and didn't own one thing of value.

I learned that hindsight is the greatest prophet. Those girls really cared about what happened to me, and they were relative strangers. But when I walked into their meeting the evening of March 27, 1996, I was welcomed with open arms. They were so excited to see me.

This meeting was not just for the girls in the house. It was a women's meeting, and there were about twenty-five women in attendance. I only knew the ten from work. But by the end of evening after hearing many of their stories, I knew this was where I belonged. Even in the brief time they had to share, I heard parts of my story in many of them. Some had been sober a few months, some many years, and other just a few days. But they had each other. They had somewhere to go where they could talk honestly about their feelings. This to me was incredible. I was sobbing by the end of the evening.

I stayed there when the meeting ended, and two of the girls spoke to the director who lived in residency there but did not attend the meetings. She was in her office. I didn't exactly know what the girls were doing, but at 10 p.m. that evening, they introduced me to the director. We spoke briefly, and she asked me if I thought I was ready to admit I was an alcoholic and to live in that house. Of course I said yes to everything, and she told me to come back the following afternoon to be interviewed and do all the paperwork.

I went for that interview. Unfortunately, they had quite a waiting list. I left discouraged, but I knew when an opening was available I would fill it.

On Friday, the director, Mary, called me at work.

"Hi, Roni, it's Mary. How would you like to move in Monday?"

"I would love to."

I was jumping up and down and hooting and hollering, and all the other girls came over to join in my craziness. They knew what that phone call was about. They were the ones who pleaded with Mary to put my name at the top of the list.

That phone call was better than winning a billion-dollar lottery. For the very first time in I don't know how many years, I had made a decision that would forever improve my life. In fact, those girls gave me back my life. That decision has continued to pay the highest possible dividends even to the present time and will continue as long as I don't pick up a drink.

The girls were so excited that I had agreed to take that first step. I still had reservations about my decision, but not for the reason you might think. I just wasn't comfortable with the fact these were not women, they were all young girls. There wasn't one girl even close to my age. I was fifty-three. Even the director was much younger than I was.

Dana was going away for the weekend. Of course she was happy knowing I'd be out of her apartment by Monday. So Andre came over, and we spent the weekend together. We went to the storage unit Sunday afternoon so I could get some of my belongings. There were only a few essentials I needed.

Monday morning he kissed me good-bye and wished me luck. We wouldn't be allowed to see one another for at least a month.

There really hadn't been any need to be concerned over the age difference. Age meant nothing in that house. And being honest, I don't always act my age. Immediately after work, on April 1, 1996, I walked into The House (which has to remain nameless).

All the girls rushed out to my car to help me bring my things in. I was put in a room with two other girls.

Three hours later, I was sitting at the dinner table with my coworkers, and for six months I lived with these women and worked with them every day.

Even the pajama parties I went to in high school weren't as much fun as that first night and all the nights following.

For someone like me who had put a wall around herself for so many years, I was now a part of an environment completely alien to anything I knew, and it felt wonderful. For the first time in years, I was included, I was welcomed, and people really cared *about me.* I was a part of a special group. I was no longer outside the circle.

The first month was awesome. I heard about the miracles. I was hearing about surrender. I was hearing about God. I was learning so much.

For the first time in my life, I felt God's presence and knew his favor. The fear that had become a part of my very being began to dissipate, and I felt safe. Living with those girls was an awesome experience. I was catching glimpses of what my life was like back at the time when my kids were growing up. It wasn't just the glimpses; it was feeling the feelings from fifteen years prior. It wasn't some silly wish to turn back the clock. I was seeing the possibility of sometime soon baking a cake or buying a new outfit. Silly little things that most people take for granted. I knew I would be able to live my life without picking up a drink. I knew the day would come when I could wake up without my first thoughts being about a drink. I could do that with God's help. I felt so good both physically and emotionally.

Five new firsts for me in The House: Structure, the sincere desire to help other people, telling the truth, taking responsibility for my actions, and being accountable to someone else. These things hadn't been a part of my life for a long time.

I knew what structure was while I was in prison. But this was far different. Here I had the choice to walk out. There were no locks.

It was heaven to know I had a place to put my head at night, it was heaven to wake up and go to a job, and it was heaven arriving home from work with all the girls and immediately doing our chores. The opportunity to have time to rest or read before dinner was so new to me. To walk into a dining room and have this wonderful dinner prepared for me was beyond awesome. I couldn't even remember the last time someone had made a meal for me. And now it was being done every night.

I was really free from the bondage of self. Everything was out of *my* control, and in this situation that was the best thing that had happened to me in eons. It was truly a gift straight from God. The ability to let go and trust. To honestly look in the mirror and admit my life had become unmanageable was an incredible experience.

That magical and marvelous word was back in my life: *Hope.*

That was the greatest miracle. I had given up so many times. I had lost so much. I honestly don't think that word had ever been a thought in my mind. Despair, depression, and desperation yes, but not *hope.*

There were house rules and one was strictly enforced: return to the house immediately after work. There were only two of us that had cars. However, I had to give my keys to the director for one week. We only lived about a mile from work, so we walked. As I'm writing this I'm chuckling to myself thinking of those first weeks. We had to be up at 5:00 a.m. We each had twenty minutes to shower, and if we didn't get in there at our scheduled time, oh well, we didn't shower. I loved every minute of it.

The camaraderie, having coffee together. There was one girl that read all of our horoscopes as we gulped down our breakfast. I, who couldn't get out of bed without a struggle, was now jumping out of the bed and loving the walk to work. The job I hated a month prior became an event to look forward to.

Every day upon returning to the house I had to complete my scheduled chore. Every room was vacuumed daily. The bathrooms were cleaned every day. Our bedrooms had to be squeaky clean.

The chores were rotated weekly. The big once-a-week chores were done on Saturday morning. No one left the house until they were done. I kid you not when I tell you we had to empty every single thing out of the kitchen cabinets and scrub them inside and outside. The refrigerator had to be completely emptied and scrubbed. I'm talking about a huge kitchen and refrigerator and freezer.

Two girls were responsible for making dinner for one week in a row. The menu was chosen for us. I couldn't believe the donations of food and clothing that came into that house. We'd get a dozen huge cans of tuna, so we had to make tuna casserole one night. Having been Suzie Homemaker in my previous life, I was thrilled when it was my turn in the kitchen. I enjoyed it and we had a blast doing it.

I remember the excitement of being chosen to go food shopping with the assistant director every week. It was just a fun thing to do. Imagine going into a supermarket and choosing whatever item (within reason) you wanted and putting it in the cart and having someone else pay for it. Of course we had the freedom to buy whatever we wanted and pay for it. As soon as we pulled up to the front door, the girls would make a mad dash out, and the bags would be in the kitchen and emptied in no time.

Everything we did was fun.

We worked on commission, and it didn't matter whether we had a good week or a bad week, we had to contribute our share of $100. Many of us were still paying long after we left.

When I celebrated my first ninety days sober, I knew it was no coincidence that I had found this job. God had a reason for keeping me alive. I learned to smile again and to laugh. My tears were now tears of joy.

A lot of the girls had lost contact with family. So Easter became a very special day. We each contributed one of our special recipes, and we were allowed to go do our own grocery shopping. We had a blast. We baked a turkey, a ham, sweet potatoes with marshmallows, baked macaroni, vegetables, and rolls and much more. Lots of pies. A few of the girls had family close by, and they joined us.

Fourth of July we had a big barbeque, and Chad and his girlfriend joined us. He was thrilled to see how happy I was. The house was beautiful. It was a ranch with a huge living room and dining room. It had four bedrooms. The garage had been converted into a big finished room with six beds. There was also a washer and dryer in there. The whole place was so cool. They had a big covered patio. There was no smoking allowed in the house, so we spent a lot of free time on that patio.

That was about the only good thing that came out of my New Year's stunt. Because of the damage I had done to my lungs, I had to quit smoking. But I'd still sit out on the patio with the other girls.

Nine months later, I moved out of the recovery home and into my own apartment. Andre and I continued to see one another, and he came over quite often. But my focus had changed, and I knew in order to remain sober, I had to reorganize my priorities. There could be no doubt that God had set me on the path to AA and the people in AA had brought me back to God.

I started to attend services at a nondenominational church, which was quite different than what I had grown up in. There was no altar. The pastor gave a forty-five-minute sermon. There had to be around seven hundred people at each of the three services. They had a large choir and a lot of singing. It was very uplifting and catchy. The sermon was long, but I was enthralled with his insight. Obviously, he had great knowledge of the Bible. But the fact was I knew nothing about the Bible, and I was intrigued by his analogies to everyday common occurrences. There were times he talked about people with addictions or people who drank, but he never once said anything in a negative manner. Often times I was mesmerized with how many of his messages spoke directly to me. A few times I thought he actually knew me personally. I wanted to hear more. There was no lightning bolt moment of revelation. It was just down-to-earth teachings from the Bible.

When Monday morning rolled away, I couldn't wait to tell the girls in work about my new church. I was in awe of what I had heard and began sharing it with the other girls. Little by little things unfolded, and I started to see some connections to the twelve steps and how they related to the pastor's sermon. Slowly the interest of some of the girls was piqued, and a few started to go to church with me. It was great.

I went to at least five AA meetings a week. There, I could talk about my past, and there was no judgment. Miraculously, the burden was lifted.

Andre was thrilled at the changes that had taken place in me and continued to be my greatest supporter.

"To have suffered much is like knowing many languages: It gives the sufferer access to many more people." That is AA in a nutshell. Addiction causes immense suffering and ridicule. We are aware of the hurt we've caused our families, friends, and society. We are so overburdened with self-loathing and guilt that it's impossible to put the drink or the drug down without the support of each other.

As Lewis Meyer puts it so succinctly,

> It is the only place I know where status means nothing. Nobody fools anybody else. Everyone is here because he or she made a slobbering mess of his or her life and is trying to put the pieces back together again … I have attended thousands of church meetings, lodge meetings, brotherhood meetings—yet I have never found the kind of love I find at AA. For one small hour the high and mighty descend and the lowly rise. The leveling that results is what people mean when they use the word fellowship. They come to AA because they believe that there, grace flows.
>
> [Brennan Manning. *The Gentle Revolutionaries.* (Denville: Dimension, 1976), 66.]

We admit our powerlessness, we turn our will and our lives over to God, and we humbly ask him to remove our shortcomings. In humility, we openly and honestly share our experiences, our strength, and our hope with others and to the newcomers. This is how I serve God for his sake alone.

No other organization has the same common denominator to bond its participants together that AA has. Even churches may follow the same basic beliefs, but the beliefs are many and varied.

We must detach from the past. That's not to say we want to forget it. But to live in the past is a worse prison than I was in at CIW. There is no release date from the liquid prison. There is no release for the mind that refuses to leave the past where it belongs, behind us.

HIS SILENCE

The long distance phone call I received in October of 1997 would leave me shattered and haunt me for years.

"We just got the results of Patrick's biopsy," Mom said. "It's malignant."

I don't recall one word of our conversation after hearing those two words. I was numb. Five minutes later, she was still talking and giving me all the details of what lay ahead.

"Mom, can I talk to him, please?" She transferred the phone.

"Patrick, I'm so sorry," I said.

Patrick lived in New Jersey. I lived in California. We were three thousand miles apart. Still, his voice begged for some words of comfort, words my mind was incapable of forming. It was a crushing and devastating blow. Patrick was my brother and a Roman Catholic priest. The operation he would undergo to remove the tumor also meant excision of his larynx, which would leave him unable to speak.

The hours following that phone call left me stunned and unable to sleep. I went into work the next day but asked to leave at two o'clock. I wanted to go to the nearby park, just to walk around the lake and be alone. About a mile before the park, I ran into a detour and realized the park was closed due to construction. I followed the detour signs, and down the road a short distance was another sign pointing to the Japanese Gardens. It had to be a mirage.

"How long have the gardens been here?" I asked the gatekeeper.

"Thirty years," he said. "You're lucky we're open today. We've been closed for months. They do a lot of filming here."

No, I wasn't lucky. I knew the person who directed me there had it opened especially for me that day.

For the next three hours, I was alone in that secret place, breathing in the magnificence of the gardens and gazing in awe as the lilies floated along the ponds. I sat on the wooden floor of the beautiful tea house and meditated. The sounds of the waterfall and trickling brook hypnotized me. I cried. I prayed. But most of all, I kept asking God, "Why? Why Patrick?" He would jump out of bed at a moment's notice to go pray for the sick and dying. His greatest joy was preaching sermons about the Lord.

It had only been a year since I had started attending church on a regular basis. I wanted so much to share with Patrick my joy of having the Lord in my life.

Driving home, I thanked God for leading me to the Gardens and the quiet time I had needed for reflection.

Two weeks passed quickly. I went to Universal Studios after work the day of Patrick's surgery. I needed to be alone and escape into the fantasy world of Hollywood. Patrick was a big movie buff. He could recall every movie that appeared on the silver screen and who starred in it. Movies had been our life when growing up in the 1950s.

Five minutes after joining the guided tour, I caught a glimpse of the house we watched on TV for years in *Leave it to Beaver*. The perfect family that the whole world tried to emulate. Not only was the house a façade, the family was too.

A short time later, we passed the house where Norman Bates sat doubling as his mother in *Psycho*. Just thinking of Janet Leigh in that shower scene still sends quivers down my spine. But as I left Universal, I was faced with something more chilling and a fear far more real.

Driving home, I thanked God once again for sending me to the only place that could divert my thoughts for a few hours. The tour sparked memories that brought both smiles and giggles. The tears flowed as I arrived home.

At eight o'clock, the call came.

"Hi, Roni, it's Mom," she said. "Patrick is out of surgery and doing fine. We spoke to the doctor. He assured us the operation went well and they were able to remove all of the cancer."

"Oh, thank God. What about the larynx?" I asked.

"Unfortunately, they had to remove it," she said.

I felt like I was suspended in time; that tiny ray of hope was gone. Our fear was now a reality. We would never hear him laugh or speak again. I would never hear him say my name, but he was alive and the cancer was removed.

Patrick would be staying at my parents' home, since he was unable to care for himself. He had other serious medical problems that required more than my eighty-year-old parents could provide. My first instinct was to suggest to the family the need to hire private duty nurses.

I did offer to take a temporary leave of absence and return to help. Having worked as a surgical nurse for years, I was quite familiar with the mechanics of the equipment he would need, along with his follow-up care.

On Thursday, two days before Patrick was to be discharged, my mother called.

"Hi, Roni. We need you to come back."

"How soon?" I asked.

"Well, he's coming home Saturday."

The following day I requested an indefinite leave of absence.

Saturday morning, I called Andre and told him I was leaving for New Jersey. He was aware of the situation and assured me that I was doing the right thing. I didn't know how I was going to get through this without him. Andre had helped me through two years of insanity due to my drinking, and he had remained very supportive when I made the decision to sign myself into a recovery home. I now had eighteen months of sobriety and was enjoying every minute of it.

My flight arrived at JFK at ten o'clock Sunday evening. It was bitter cold, and I had just missed the last shuttle to the main terminal. There I stood on the tarmac with the sleet and snow coming down, not having a clue what to do. I had five suitcases and no jacket. Leaving my luggage on the sidewalk, I went in search of a phone.

"Hi, Mom, it's Roni," I said. "I'm at the airport. I missed the last shuttle bus. Is it okay if I take a cab? I don't have any money on me."

"Yes," she said curtly.

The drive took about an hour and a half. It was a very emotional ride. It had been more than twenty years since I had been anywhere near this area. It was like stepping back in time as we drove across the Verrazano Bridge with reminders of happier times. Some areas had changed, but seeing the strip malls and the crazy U-turns, called jug handles, on the highway left no doubt I was back in New Jersey.

As we passed Newark Airport, I knew we were only a short distance from my parents' home. My stomach started doing the same flip-flops it had done an hour before as the plane descended. I was suddenly overcome with feelings of apprehension, thoughts of severe criticism, but mostly an overwhelming dread that I had made a terrible mistake by coming here.

As the cab pulled up breaking my reverie, I said, "Please, God, help me."

As I walked up to the enclosed porch, my anxiety increased. It was the house in which I had grown up but not a home that gave me a warm and cozy feeling. It was a place that made friends and relatives feel comfortable and welcome. But for me, it was a house devoid of love and nurturing. The only memories I had were of severe discipline and the reverberating sound of my father issuing edicts.

Stepping into the living room, the first thing I saw was Patrick sitting in the cane back chair. He had aged twenty years, and I was stunned to see the once clean-shaven priest with a full gray beard. He could barely lift his head, and when he did, all I saw was a vacant stare. My heart sank.

My father was already in bed. My mother and I sat in the living room with Mary Elizabeth (his nurse) and made small talk. Patrick just listened. The conversations in my head had already started: "You'll never hear another one of his sermons or share the joy of his laughter." The joking and teasing that were so much a part of our relationship were now history. It was heartrending to see the glee and joviality replaced with such sadness.

I excused myself and said goodnight. As I passed Patrick's room, I glanced in and was surprised by the array of medical supplies, a nebulizer, two oxygen tanks, and the two suctioning machines. There were boxes piled six deep in the corner of his room filled with dressings and tubings and cannulas. There were two large cartons containing dozens of trach kits. The top of his dresser was lined with varying sizes of amber and clear prescription containers. There were bags of little plastic bullets filled with saline to squirt into the opening in his throat.

The second nurse, Trish, came on duty at seven o'clock Monday morning. Patrick came into the living room for a while. He just sat in the chair leaning forward with his elbows on his knees and his head resting in his hands. I wanted so much to know what he was thinking. I wanted to weep as I sat and watched him. That scene filled me with guilt as it triggered memories of childhood hatred and envy for all the love that I so desperately sought but was instead showered on him.

That evening, my brother Dennis, his wife, Carol, and their three kids came to visit. We agreed that the nurses should remain for another two days.

When Mary Elizabeth arrived at ten o'clock that evening, Patrick was napping. "I have a little story to tell you," she said. "When I arrived Saturday and realized your brother was a priest, I was really nervous! I told him I wasn't Catholic, and you know what he did?"

"What?"

"He wrote, 'No, not yet!'"

We all had a much-needed chuckle over that. Patrick still had his sense of humor.

An hour later, he came into the living room with us.

"So, Father Pat, you think you're going to convert Miss Mary Elizabeth here?" I asked.

I saw the sparkle in his eye, which spoke loud and clear, "Just you wait and see!"

Thursday, the designated day to pass the torch of caregiver, had arrived. The transition went very smoothly. Unfortunately, there hadn't been enough time for Patrick to do his miracle conversion on Nurse Mary Elizabeth.

He was eating a little better. The first day went very well. At eleven o'clock that evening, I cleaned his trach and changed his dressing. He gestured that he would be okay and I should go to bed.

At three o'clock, I suddenly woke to the sound of Patrick ringing the bell. I sprinted into his room. He was sitting on the edge of the bed holding the entire trach in his hand. I recognized the depth of his emotion because it matched my own. At that moment, he ceased to be my brother. He was my parents' son and a man of God, and I started praying as I never prayed in my life.

Patrick remained calm as I very gently maneuvered the trach into the opening in his throat and eased it as far as it would go without any resistance. I held my breath for the next five minutes, terrified that the trach might be blocking his airway. I was the one holding the trach, but I know who had guided it into place.

There remained a silence of words between us, but Patrick's eyes spoke volumes.

That moment would forever bond us with gratitude toward God that was palpable.

Patrick had a clipboard, but he made no attempt to converse with us. He wouldn't join us for meals.

"Well, Patrick, how about we watch *Gone With the Wind?*" I asked.

I was somewhat taken aback when he shook his head no. That was his favorite movie.

"If you change your mind, join us in the living room," I said. Reluctantly, he did come in later to watch it.

The following two weeks were spent taking him to various doctors. Dr. Wald, the surgeon, was pleased with his progress and assured Patrick that his prognosis for the future was excellent.

Our next trip was to the radiologist, who told Patrick he would need eight weeks of radiation.

The third week in November, Patrick had an appointment with the kidney specialist. The doctor did a thorough examination, along with lab tests. Afterward, we went into his office, where he told us Patrick was close to complete renal shutdown and would need dialysis. No one gave a more convincing display of nonchalance than Patrick.

My parents were devastated.

"This isn't the end of the world," I said. "Thousands of people incorporate it into their schedule, and they live very long and productive lives."

The following day was Thanksgiving. It had been a tradition for years that my parents and Patrick would go to Carol's parents for dinner.

"Hey, Patrick, are you up to it?" I asked.

"Yeah, I'd like to go," he wrote.

We went to bed around eleven o'clock that evening. I could hear Patrick tossing and turning. At two o'clock, I went into his room. He was sitting up.

"Patrick, please be honest. What's the matter?" I asked.

"I'm having trouble breathing," he wrote.

Twenty minutes later, he was in an ambulance being rushed to the hospital. My dad and I remained at the hospital until Patrick was admitted.

"How about after Dad and I get some rest, we go back to the hospital for a while and then spend the afternoon with the family as planned?" I suggested.

"Sure," Dad said.

By the time we arrived at the hospital, Patrick was resting comfortably. We stayed for two hours and then joined the others for dinner. We had an enjoyable afternoon. We needed time away from the crisis, and these were the perfect people to be with.

When we arrived at the hospital the following morning, Patrick was in the dialysis unit. I went down to see how he was doing. What a surprise! He had color in his face, and the bloating was greatly reduced. The miracle was reading his lips say, "I'm starved!"

"Patrick, you look *great*," I said.

I was truly excited. Even without wings, I flew back to Patrick's room where my parents were waiting. "You have your son back. He's going to be just fine."

A short time later, Patrick was back in his bed enjoying his dinner. We left in better spirits than we had been in for weeks.

The following week, the radiation treatments started. He was doing very well, and we were anticipating his being discharged. But another three weeks passed, and Patrick was no closer to coming home than he was when he had arrived there. Meanwhile, there was no physical therapy being done, and he was growing more and more stiff, along with experiencing severe cramps in his legs and feet. I would massage his calves and feet while I was there, which seemed to help, but only temporarily.

I drove to the cancer center to borrow the electrolarynx. This is a device similar to a handheld microphone, and, when held against the throat, it picks up the vibrations of the words that are being mouthed and translates them into sound. With a great deal of practice, one becomes quite fluent in learning to speak through it. That seemed to be our last hope of getting Patrick to start communicating with us.

He would work with the speech therapist every few days, but he never picked it up or made any attempt to use it once she left.

A few days later, while we were visiting, the doctor stopped in to see Patrick. When he was through examining him, he asked me to step out into the hall.

"Roni, your brother has about five months to live," he said. I heard him, but I didn't want to believe him.

"What are you talking about?" I asked. "He's improved one hundred percent with the dialysis. Besides, the surgeon and the radiologist have both assured us that the cancer was removed."

"I don't foresee the possibility of his lasting very long with all his other medical problems," he said.

He noted, "Your parents are very frail and obviously anxious to see him get well. I don't want to give your family any false hopes."

I now had the burdensome task of telling my parents the son they loved dearly would not live to see his fifty-eighth birthday. I wanted the ground to open and swallow me.

The following morning, when I came downstairs, my father took one look at me and knew something was very wrong.

"What's the matter? Is it about Patrick?" he asked.

"C'mon, let's the three of us go into the TV room," I said.

I told them word for word what the doctor told me, adding, "I'm sure he's wrong."

"It was all for nothing," my father said. I was crushed by the weight of those five words and the expression of sadness in his eyes. My mother sat there shaking her head. "I'm not surprised," she said in a very quiet voice.

We continued to visit with Patrick daily. He was eating better but kept losing weight. He was not making any effort to work with the speaker device. He did start to get out of bed and sit in the chair for a few hours.

With him unable to speak, my mother almost blind, and my father extremely hard of hearing, our visits with Patrick were very trying. At night, I would spend an hour preparing things to discuss with him, just to keep the conversation flowing and to cheer him up.

There were times this same scene was quite humorous, reminding me of "Charades." I'd ask Patrick a question, he'd write his response, and my mother wanted to know immediately what he wrote. There were a lot of eyes rolling between Patrick and me. I kept expecting to hear Alan Funt say, "Guess what? You're on *Candid Camera!*"

Patrick and I had some awesome conversations about God and spirituality. On Sundays, I would tell him about the sermon I had heard at church. That led into a wonderful discussion. I told him what Alcoholics Anonymous had taught me about surrendering to God's will. Patrick had worked with various recovery groups throughout the years, so he in turn shared his experiences and agreed that it was a wonderful program. We compared our little spiritual quotes and stories. I treasured those moments!

He was very happy to see that I had come to know the Lord and that my life had taken on some meaningful purpose.

> For the lips of a priest ought to preserve knowledge, and from his mouth men should seek instruction—because he is a messenger of the Lord Almighty.
>
> Malachi 2:7 (NIV)

We also had fun discussing the change in movies since we were kids, back in the dinosaur age.

Dennis visited him every day, and my sister-in-law came with the kids as often as possible.

One particular day, Patrick was sitting in a chair when we arrived, and I noticed a new lump on his neck, the size of a walnut. I could taste the bile rising in my throat as my mind started to run.

"Patrick, are you aware of the lump on your neck?" I asked.

He reached up to feel it and shook his head no.

"Haven't any of the nurses who wash you commented on it?"

Again, he shook his head no.

I went out to the nurses' station and asked his nurse to please come in and look at it. She contacted the doctor immediately, and he came in that afternoon and ordered a biopsy.

It was four days before Christmas, and this had clearly squashed any hope we had of Patrick being home for the holidays.

Chad was flying in from California, and Eric and his wife, Kim, were driving up from D.C. It was to be the first time all of us would be together.

Two days before Christmas, the doctor called.

"The cancer has metastasized," he said.

"Has Patrick been told?"

"Yes."

Eric and Kim arrived two hours later. We ate dinner and just hung around.

Dennis, Carol, and the kids were at the house when Chad arrived the following morning.

A short time later, we all left for the hospital. It was both a tearful and joyful time. I caught the sparkle in Patrick's eyes as he watched each one of his nephews and nieces hovering about his bed. It was a Kodak moment, and I had the camera propped and ready to shoot.

Once again, you could see Patrick as the proud uncle. He'd been the uncle who had loved to take his nephews and nieces around church introducing them to his parishioners.

It was truly a bittersweet reunion.

Christmas day, with presents in hand, we all went to visit Patrick again. Turkey sandwiches were his favorite, so Mom made two for him topped with homemade cranberry sauce. We were thankful to find him in good spirits.

We continued to visit daily, rotating so he was able to spend time with everyone. Before we knew it, the time arrived for Chad to return to California. The miracle of Christmas had once again been displayed, even if only for a few days. The sadness had been lifted as we watched Patrick's delight at having been surrounded by his family.

"Mom, how would you like to visit with us for a few days?" my son asked.

"I would love to," I replied. "Let me discuss it with Grandma, and I'll make a few calls to arrange for them to be driven to the hospital."

"Sounds great," Eric said.

He and Kim returned to D.C. the following day, with the plans finalized for me to visit with them the first week of January.

The following few days zipped by, and suddenly I was on the train heading for D.C. The three-hour trip gave me the much-needed time to unwind and think about the remaining details before I returned to California in two weeks.

Eric picked me up at Union Station, and we drove to their apartment, where Kim had a wonderful chicken enchilada dinner all prepared. It felt like a little bit of heaven to be with my son and daughter-in-law in their apartment and to have this private time with them. After touring the Smithsonian Institute, the FBI Building, and the Holocaust Museum, we had lunch at the Hard Rock Café. Sunday, they took me for a wonderful brunch. Those four days would fill my scrapbook pages with joyful memories. I boarded the train with a renewed energy and a long overdue peacefulness.

Two weeks later, Patrick was transferred to a rehabilitation center.

My last visit with Patrick was very difficult.

"Well, Patrick, have I made up to you for some of the bratty things I did to you as a kid?" I asked.

He laughed his silent laugh.

"A hundred times over," he wrote on a piece of paper.

We were down to the last few minutes, and it was tough. I could see the sadness in Patrick's eyes. I wanted so much to believe he would survive.

Through tear-blurred eyes, I said, "I love you."

Patrick signed, "I love you."

PATRICK GOES HOME
TO THE LORD

I kept in touch with my family daily as the cancer continued to ravage Patrick's body. The first week of March, he was readmitted to the hospital.

It was decided, along with Patrick's permission, to cease all treatment.

Once a person stops dialysis treatment, the longest he can live is four days, possibly five.

Dennis, Todd, and I agreed someone should speak to Patrick and tell him it was okay to let go. Thursday, March 26, would be his last dialysis treatment. The final countdown had begun. Wednesday evening Dennis went to the hospital, where he expressed all of our feelings collectively.

"Patrick, you've been struggling for so long," Dennis said. "It's time for you to rest. We'll take good care of Mom and Dad. We all love you very much." A few hours later, Patrick went into a coma.

Sunday morning, my parents were at the hospital. They left at noon knowing that Dennis and Carol were on their way. In those few minutes, Patrick took his last breath and went to be with the Lord.

I was alone when the call came from my mother. I thought I had prepared myself for this; however, it was still a shock to hear the words, "Patrick's gone."

I recalled the earlier conversation with Patrick's doctor. "Five months," he'd said. Patrick didn't even make it that long.

The church had sole responsibility for all the arrangements. Patrick was given a beautiful farewell. The funeral parlor was packed all day and all evening. Two men from the Knights of Columbus stood honor guard in full dress uniform of gold and blue at both ends of the coffin.

The pastor invited the entire family for a homemade dinner of pot roast, mashed potatoes, and vegetables, along with dessert. The aromas as we walked into the rectory were comforting. There was a sense of warmth and peace, as though Patrick was still with us. We enjoyed the reversal of roles, as the priests had become the servers for that one evening.

The following morning, Patrick was moved to the church. The long circular driveway was lined with the children from his school, and the flag was at half-mast. Tears were brimming as I recalled being that age and how sad I was when our pastor had died. Now these children were feeling that same sadness. His body remained for viewing in the church until Friday morning. The lines were continuous, and the hundreds who came praised him for all the wonderful things he had done for people.

Friday morning was the funeral mass. The pastor

invited everyone back to the church hall for a luncheon after the cemetery.

Patrick was given all the respect and reverence he so deserved.

Returning home took some adjusting. I went back to work immediately, and Andre and I resumed our relationship. I was going to my AA meetings, and within a few weeks, I was back to my normal routine.

The following six weeks flew by, and suddenly it was time to start packing again. Chad and I were flying back to attend Eric's graduation from Georgetown University. We were going to spend a few days with my parents before the trip to D.C.

Mom was unable to attend due to her failing eyesight. My aunt Betty spent the weekend with her. My dad was very excited about going to his grandson's graduation.

Monday, we were all up bright and early. We could not have asked for a more beautiful day. The ambience of Georgetown University is magnificent, and watching the graduates marching in with the navy blue and purple attire was breathtaking. As I studied each one walking up to receive his or her diploma, I wondered if it were possible that another student had gone through what Eric had in order to reach this moment. Just then, his name was called, and the adjective "Cum Laude" was announced. No mother could have been prouder.

Afterward, my dad took us all out to dinner at a nice restaurant in Union Station, and then we boarded the train.

Three weeks after returning to California, I received a call from my mother. My father had suffered a heart attack, during which time they discovered he had advanced cancer of the esophagus.

DECISION TO MOVE BACK TO NEW JERSEY

History was repeating itself, and a decision had to be made. If I returned to New Jersey to take care of my father, it would mean moving there permanently. My mother could not care for him with her worsening glaucoma and very limited eyesight. She could get around the house and cook but nothing more.

"Roni, I don't know what I'm going to do. Dad is starting to lose his memory. At four o'clock this morning, he got dressed and was leaving to take the car to the repair shop. When I tried to keep him from leaving, he fell, and I couldn't get him up."

"Mom, do you want me to move back?"

"I think it would be a good idea, but I don't want any trouble," she said.

What did she mean by that remark?

I'd picked up on my brother Dennis's indifference when I stayed at my parents' during Patrick's illness. I also knew that his drinking was out of control—something I never knew prior. It would take another few months before I realized the depth of his resentment.

Had I known the story of the Prodigal Son, I would have better understood that my return to care for Patrick was seen as an intrusion by other family members. The scarlet sister returns as the rescuer. I had no clue that the ramifications of my second return would be my undoing.

"We're hoping you can be here by the middle of July," my mother announced.

I almost dropped the phone. It was now July 3. Once she had made up her mind, she wanted me there yesterday and would not let up on me for the next four weeks. I had an apartment full of furniture. Some had to be sold, some given away, some taken to Goodwill, some put in storage. There were items and clothes to be packed and shipped to New Jersey. I had a car to sell, insurance to cancel. I was still working and had to give notice.

Andre took eighteen boxes and had them shipped from work, which saved me more than $450. Lastly he moved what little belongings I still owned into a storage unit.

He and I went out one night with Chad and Dana. It was an emotional evening; however, I knew I'd see Chad during the holidays.

The following week came the moment I dreaded. Andre and I had been together for more than nine years, and I knew in my heart we would never see one another again. I was entering into a new phase of my life.

It was very difficult saying good-bye to Andre. We were parting as lovers but would always be friends. He drove me to the airport, and we agreed that it would be better that he just dropped me off. I left California with

Andre very much on my mind and a piece of my heart in his.

I was emotionally spent by the time I got on the plane.

When I arrived at Newark airport and got into the cab, I took a quantum leap back in time. It was ten o'clock in the evening when I arrived at my parents' house. The three of us sat talking for a short while, and then I carried my luggage up to my room and we all went to bed. The boxes Andre shipped had already arrived.

My father was having a great deal of difficulty swallowing. Mornings he would go into the TV room and read the newspaper or watch television. Inevitably, he'd fall asleep.

"That's all he does is read the paper and fall asleep," Mom said.

"Mom, he's eighty-seven, he has cancer, a heart condition, and he's in pain, so please let's just leave him alone," I said.

Then she would get upset with me for defending him.

He loved his little TV room and just wanted to be left alone. She continued to nag him. I was seeing a side of her that I had never been aware of.

The date had already been scheduled for Dad to have the endoscopy at the hospital. He got through that very well.

A few days later, I noticed my mother's yearbook lying on the cocktail table. The three of us sat together while Dad went through it page by page. My parents had the most incredible memories, and they could remember more than half of the people and recall who married who and where they went to work. It was a very enjoyable hour listening to the two of them reminiscing. It was a night I would never forget.

The following week, Dad was admitted to the hospital.

I hadn't been to an AA meeting since I had arrived three weeks prior.

"Mom, I need to get to a meeting in the morning. There's one nearby at nine o'clock."

"Okay," she said.

When I got home, she carried on about how quiet the house was while I was gone and how lonely she was. I couldn't believe it. She seldom got up before 8:30; she was only alone for an hour and a half. This was not a good sign.

When we arrived at the hospital Sunday, Dad was very agitated and didn't know what was going on. He was pulling his IV out. We only stayed for about an hour.

Monday, Dad showed no improvement and had to be strapped to the bed around the clock. He didn't have a clue who I was. We still went up every day. Dennis and Carol visited daily. It was a very sad week, and I knew my mother was hurting. Dad continued to be nasty, and finally, Mom stopped talking to him altogether.

Todd arrived Friday evening. We were shocked to see the look on my father's face when he saw Todd. He was still strapped down, but he raised his head.

"Todd, when did you get here?" he asked, recognizing him instantly.

It was a good weekend. Todd, Dennis, Carol, and the kids went up together Saturday. We were all going to the diner Sunday morning for breakfast.

Dad was transported home by ambulance the following morning. He lay in the bed wide awake but completely subdued for the first few hours. Suddenly, he started to get very agitated. He sat up and kept yelling to be let out. He was shaking the side rails and trying to reach the curtains. All hell broke loose just as Dennis arrived.

"He should've never been brought home," Dennis said.

My mother was beside herself.

"You're probably right," she admitted.

There were too many people in the bedroom: my cousin, my sister-in-law, Dennis, my mother, and me. I was fed up with all the nonsense and chaos, the "Drama Junkies." They'd come in for a few hours, stir up trouble, and who's left to deal with her and my father?

This was the culmination of ten days of the family bickering over where they wanted my father to go. No one seemed capable of accepting the fact that he could not go to a nursing home. None of my dad's problems warranted that type of care, and they would not keep him in the hospital. Everyone thought they knew what was best for my dad.

Little by little, I was beginning to feel the tug of indifference. Dennis's drinking was escalating. I knew he was resenting my intrusion after all these years. In his opinion, I had no right to return and take over the care of my father. It became evident that it was me they were fighting.

There had been a rather ugly disagreement between my dad and my cousin a few weeks prior. She was insisting he should have a feeding tube put in. And my father was adamant in his decision that there would be no feeding tube. That was another issue the family thought I had instigated. Meanwhile, I had never voiced my opinion either way.

I politely asked them to leave the room. I sat on the floor out of my father's sight, just to see how long he would keep this up. Like a child, he probably could have kept it up for a few hours. I knew the rest of them were out in the kitchen thinking, *Oh, she'll never be able to do anything with him.* Quite honestly, I didn't know myself if I could. I waited about twenty minutes and made my move.

"Mr. Brennan, it's time for you to lie down," I said firmly but politely.

He continued to grip the railing like a vise. I literally had to pry his fingers off of it and, with a bit of gentle force, got him to lie down. I raised the bed and put an extra pillow under his head.

"Isn't that better?" I asked.

"Yes," he said.

A few days later, I started him on the oxygen and morphine.

Ten days later, on August 31, he passed away.

We had the wake on Wednesday and Thursday.

"I wish I could see him one more time," my mother kept repeating.

The lighting in the funeral parlor was so dim, and with her limited eyesight, she couldn't see him. When the visitation hours ended, I took off my black blazer and asked the funeral director to please place it under my father's head. The effect was exactly what my mother needed to see him, and she left content.

I gave the eulogy at the funeral mass on Friday.

We had been so devastated by Patrick's death five months prior that my father's passing really didn't have a big effect on any of us.

He was eighty-seven, and there was no way I would wish him to go on living and suffering with the type of cancer he had. His death had not affected me. I think at the time I feared living alone with my mother because of the other family members' indifference toward me. My mother and I had a very toxic relationship for as long as I could remember.

The following day the entire family, my sons, my daughter-in-law, my brothers, nephews, niece, and sister-in-law all went to a baseball game in New York, while the servant stayed home caring for Mom. No one had even asked if I'd like to go with them.

I thought going to a baseball game on the only one full day they could spend with my mother was outrageous. The fact that they had thought ahead and planned this so precisely floored me. Four of them were from out of state. It wasn't like these plans had been in motion for months. And I thought it was very unfair to my mother, who would have loved to spend that last day with them. But that was my problem. I worried too much how things affected her, while the rest were off having a good time. But she would never speak up to them. Instead she'd complain to me, and I was sick of hearing it.

They called to let me know they were on their way back from the city and Mom and I were to meet them at the diner for dinner.

By noon the following day, everyone was gone.

So began my journey of isolation and ostracism from my family.

I would get up in the morning and immediately start to serve. I'd read the St. Francis prayer, "Make me an instrument of your peace," followed by the Serenity Prayer, until I could say them backward and forward and almost drove myself crazy.

We kept busy packing Dad's clothes to give to the veterans while immersed in a ton of paperwork. I was on the phone for days with insurance companies, the Social Security office, and the bank.

Then, after months of activity, an eerie kind of silence descended upon us.

By the third week, Mom was starting to get restless. We took a ride to the shore and had lunch. It was a beautiful day, and we enjoyed sitting on the boardwalk, watching the boats coming in and out of the inlet. We could hear the boats signal to raise the bridge within a few yards of where we sat. We listened to the waves. The smell of the salt water brought back many childhood memories. My mother loved reminiscing; I listened to her and spoke when it was appropriate.

Mom had a to-do list a mile long. There was one thing on it I would have no part of, but she kept nagging and nagging me about it. It was Patrick's estate. Dennis was the executor, and with all the animosity toward me, I refused to get involved.

The cooler weather was starting to set in. Mom was feeling lonesome and couldn't understand why no one was stopping by. This only added more of a burden on me to keep her entertained. I literally spent every waking moment with her. I abhorred the cold weather and was already missing California.

Andre and I kept in touch on a regular basis. The conversations were becoming more and more difficult. He still spoke in terms of my returning.

"I miss you so much," he said.

"I miss you too, more than you'll ever know," I replied.

"When are you coming back?"

"Andre, I really don't know. With my father gone, I don't see how I could ever leave my mother," I said.

"Isn't there anyone else to care for her?"

"Unfortunately, no!"

At the time, I didn't know how wrong I was. Only in hindsight would I look back and wish that I had returned to California.

"FRIENDLY FIRE"

On the second Saturday in October, I was getting ready to go to a nine o'clock meeting.

"Why do you have to go every Saturday?" Mom asked.

"I should be going to at least three meetings a week."

"Well, what's the big deal if you miss it one time?"

I could tell that my mother did not have an understanding of how AA worked and did not wish to.

Everyone went back to their normal routines. My sister-in-law was working. My cousin who had helped my family for months had her own kids to take care of. I don't know what Dennis was doing. Things had settled down, and there really weren't any major things we needed help with. After so many months of caring for Patrick and then my father, the house was suddenly very quiet, eerily so. I know my mother was bored, and now she had all the free time to think of all the things around the house she wanted done like cleaning out the attic, cleaning out all the kitchen cabinets, and filing all her paperwork in such a manner she could read them. My father also had tons of paperwork stored in the basement. He had shelves and file cabinets overflowing with income tax returns from clients for the past twenty years. We had to get rid of them. So we spent a few hours every day tearing them up and discarding them a little at a time.

My entire day consisted of talking and reading to my mother, doing the chores, paying her bills, and taking her wherever she wished. After dinner, when I did start going to the basement to exercise, she'd be calling down to me every five minutes.

"What are you doing down there?" she asked.

"I'm exercising."

"How much longer are you going to be?"

She never gave me a moment of privacy.

"I wish Dennis would get moving on Patrick's estate," Mom said. "His car has been sitting in the driveway for months."

I finally called the DMV and was told it could be put in Mom's name before the estate was settled. They would send us the necessary forms.

I suggested that we call Dennis and give him this update. I knew the bomb was about to fall. However, there was still that little flicker of hope that he might be glad this was taken care of.

"What right do you have getting involved in this?" he barked at me.

He began yelling, "All you've done since you got back here is cause trouble! This is none of your concern!"

Then I heard the click.

He called back a few minutes later, and my mother answered. Of course, she would never defend me.

He told her he'd handle everything from here on.

I wished I had gotten on a plane the day after my father's funeral and returned to California. I did not need this abuse from Dennis. He wasn't capable of taking care of any of these things. He had lost his job and only had to say a few words before you knew he had been drinking, whether it was ten in the morning or ten in the evening. I had done the unforgivable and suggested he go to a meeting with me. This was a few weeks prior. He wasn't close to admitting he was an alcoholic.

A few weeks later, I suggested to my mother we keep my father's car.

"When I get a job, I'll pay you so much a month for it," I said.

"Oh no, that's out of the question. I don't want two cars parked in the driveway," she said. It was seven years old with only 37,000 miles on it and in perfect condition.

It was rather degrading at my age to ask permission to go to a meeting and to use the car. Suddenly, I understood why she would never let me buy that car. She'd be forced to relinquish her control over me.

Around the third week of October, I took my mother for her monthly blood test. The office was quite busy.

"Do you need any help?" I asked jokingly.

"Yes! Yes! Yes!" came the response.

A few minutes later, one of the doctor's assistants handed me an application.

"What do you think, Mom?" I asked.

She was a little hesitant, but she knew I needed a job, and it was only part time. It was for the receptionist's position. I was on cloud nine walking out of there.

As soon as we got home, I called my sons. They were very happy for me.

It was heaven to get out and meet people. Once my mother adjusted, I really believe she was happy to have those few hours alone. I began going in on the average of five hours, three days a week. I was so overwhelmed with gratitude and knew this was exactly what God wanted for me.

Dennis was furious that Mom was being left home alone. I wanted to tell him to get off his perch and come sit with her since he wasn't working, but I wouldn't dare. Dennis had a volatile temper.

These situations were very upsetting. I feared any confrontation with him. It was becoming more evident that he was having problems within his own family. I had heard a few stories of his temper at home.

About two weeks later, I asked her again about keeping Dad's car, but she refused to budge. I assumed she was going to sell it.

"Let me start paying you for Patrick's car," I suggested. "I'll give you so much a month, and I'll pay the insurance."

That was a definite no.

I just wished I'd had some forewarning before I moved. Unfortunately, I had reached the famed "Siegfried Line." I had run across no-man's land and jumped into the enemy's trench. "The Friendly Fire" most people fear was now my enemy.

Two weeks later, my mother was the legal owner of Patrick's car.

On arriving home one day, I saw my mother standing at the front door.

"Roni, sit down. I have some very upsetting news to tell you. After I ate lunch, I got a severe pain in my chest," she said. She felt better now and pleaded with me not to call the doctor or take her to the hospital.

"Mom, I'm going to do exactly what you would do if the situation were reversed," I said.

I called my brother.

"Dennis, I'm taking Mom to the hospital. She was having chest pains this afternoon."

"I'll meet you there," he said.

Her EKG was abnormal, and she had to be admitted. Two days later, she had a pacemaker inserted. I brought her home the day before Thanksgiving.

Dennis called that evening and informed my mother that his wife had packed up the kids and moved out. My mother was sitting there in the worst state of depression, and for the next five hours, all she did was talk about Dennis and Carol and how worried she was about the kids. I wanted to get in the car and drive down to my brother's and tear him apart.

Mom and I went to Carol's parents' on Thanksgiving. Carol was there with the kids. It was a difficult visit.

"Don't feel bad, Roni," Carol said. "He just went off the deep end, and you're his excuse for getting drunk."

Driving home, I thought of all the changes that had taken place in one year. Patrick was gone, my father was gone, I had moved from California to New Jersey, Andre was no longer a part of my life, my sister-in-law had left my brother, my mother now had a pacemaker, and it had taken only four months for me to become the scapegoat that would be blamed for Dennis's drinking.

I had to be the only person in the world dreading the four-day weekend.

Normality would never be attainable in the Brennan household after this. Every waking moment would be spent dissecting Dennis and his problem. Mom had to call every one of her friends and go over the whole saga in detail.

I would have lost my mind had it not been for my job. Other than my one-hour meeting Saturday morning, I had absolutely no outlet.

I had been warned by Eric and my brother Todd to stay clear of Dennis. He was full of anger and resentment toward me. Dennis took everything I did as a personal affront.

Eric had been in touch with him and made every attempt to reason with him and suggest he get help. Todd was doing the same thing, but Dennis wouldn't listen. He wanted to be in charge of everything, and he was losing all control.

"Mom, would you reconsider letting me buy Dad's car?" I asked again.

"Oh, I've decided to give it to Jason," she responded. "I discussed it with Dennis and Todd, and they agreed it should go to Jason."

I was speechless. How long this had been decided would forever remain a mystery, but, once more, the picture was clear. *Roni, you're our servant, our hostage, and our chauffeur.* Silly me to have thought I should be included in on any discussions or decisions.

I certainly had no objections to my nephew getting the car, but it made no sense. He wouldn't have his license for another year.

Unwittingly, I had begun a pattern that would cause me a lot of heartache. When I made the decision to move back, my only concern was for my parents. With my dad gone, my only concern was to care for my mother. Part of that process was shielding her from the discord between Dennis and me. I failed to see that she really didn't care about my feelings.

Chad decided to fly in from California for Christmas. Eric and Kim would also be with us for the holidays.

The atmosphere around the house was very depressing. I was killing myself getting prepared and shopping and baking, along with working. I had already spent more than $2,000 on presents for my kids and my niece and nephews. The holidays were going to be festive. I was determined.

There were only three days left until Chad arrived. I couldn't wait to greet him at the airport.

"Oh, by the way, Dennis will pick Chad up at the airport," my mother informed me.

I hadn't even warranted the respect of being asked if that was okay. No doubt Dennis would be drinking before he drove to the airport.

And, once again, I felt helpless to stand up to her or to call Dennis myself and tell him I would pick up Chad. Here I was again, attempting to keep the peace. I had thought about calling Chad and suggesting he call Dennis to tell him not to pick him up. But that would involve having to tell Chad about Dennis's problem, which I chose not to do before he arrived.

By Thursday, I was exhausted. I had been up until midnight the past three nights wrapping presents, decorating the tree, and getting all the last minute things ready.

Eric and Kim arrived at three o'clock. Dennis came with Chad around six o'clock. Everyone enjoyed dinner. Dennis had adapted very well to his self-pity role and successfully accomplished his goal, which was not to say a word to the wretched sister. He left immediately after we had our coffee and dessert.

We opened presents in the hopes of forcing a more cheerful atmosphere.

Christmas morning, we got up early and had breakfast, and I went to church. Dennis was there when I got back.

Carol arrived with the kids and her parents at eleven o'clock. We exchanged presents, but Dennis remained silent. His oldest son wouldn't even speak to him. They left around two o'clock.

By four o'clock, the ham was ready to be sliced, and Kim and I were starting to put the food on the table.

"I'm leaving," Dennis announced.

My mother completely lost it.

"Please, Dennis, don't leave without having dinner with us," she pleaded.

"No, I'm not in the mood to eat," he said.

Thirty seconds later, he was out the door. Eric went after him. Twenty minutes later, I put the ham back in the oven and covered the rest of the food. The spirit and mood was ruined, and my son was trying to reason with someone who could not care less about anyone but himself.

He finally came back in with Eric after a half an hour of coaxing, but he left immediately after he ate.

We cleaned up, and Kim suggested we play Trivial Pursuit.

"Thank you, God, and thank you, Kim," I said to myself.

An hour later, we were actually laughing, and the unpleasantness of the past month was forgotten.

Eric and Kim left the following day.

I got all of twenty minutes alone with Chad before he flew back to California. Dennis drove him to the airport.

The holidays were over, and I was thrilled to be back at work.

A few days later, my mother informed me Dennis had called.

"He asked me if he could move in with us," she said.

"Really? What did you tell him?" I asked.

"I told him to come up tomorrow, and we'd discuss it," she said. "How do you feel about it?"

"I have no problem with it."

He had moved into a motel six weeks prior, and that was not a good place for a recovering alcoholic to be.

I knew she had already told him yes. Otherwise, why would he be coming the next day? It was her house, and, no doubt, we both felt he would more likely keep to his agreement to get help while living with us.

When he arrived the following day, I said, "Dennis, this is now my home, not in a monetary sense, but I gave up everything when I moved here. If there is any trouble, I don't want to be the one forced to move out."

My life's belongings, which consisted of a microwave, a vacuum cleaner, kitchen utensils, photo albums, and personal items, were still shoved inside a small storage unit in California. I had no life insurance or pension, no stocks or bonds or mutual funds or IRA, and no savings account. I had nothing, not even a car.

What I did have was an overwhelming fear of not having a place to live. I'd been homeless more times than I cared to remember, and I wasn't about to let Dennis's resentment or problems carry over into my life.

My mother discussed what her stipulations were, and the three of us agreed to be respectful of each other. Dennis had already started counseling and was attending AA meetings. Most importantly, there would be no smoking in the house.

Once he moved in, it was good to have him there. Mom was enjoying the camaraderie and listening to us joke around and tease one another.

Two weeks later, he asked Mom if it was okay if he had one cigarette in the morning and another after dinner in the basement. She, of course, agreed.

It was only a matter of time before he became the "Cellar Dweller" he had been for years and was down there smoking like a chimney. He set up a table to use as his desk, and he had a cell phone. And every moment he was home (which was quite often since he still was not working), he escaped to his little haven.

It wasn't even a year since we had lost Patrick and Dad to cancer. I had to have a resection on my lungs following the suicide attempt. Mom had congestive heart failure, along with a recent pacemaker insertion. Then, to add to all this, a week prior, she felt a lump on her neck. After having a biopsy, it was discovered she had Hodgkin's. Yet, at my mere mention of Dennis smoking, she got ticked off at me.

For the following six weeks, I drove home every day at lunch time and took Mom to the hospital for her radiation treatments.

It was now going on six months since I had moved back, and during that entire time, Dennis had not worked.

Fortunately, Mom was not in any pain. However, her demands had become intolerable and physically impossible to meet. Every time I went shopping, she'd want certain items from one grocery store and some from another store. I wanted to scream every time I went into the store.

Our next project was getting all the income tax information prepared and submitted to her accountant.

Before I could do my income taxes, I needed to get forms from California. Unfortunately, neither Andre or my other friend Steve nor my son Chad could find them anywhere. All three of them lived in California and were trying to locate them.

"What's so difficult about getting some forms and putting them in the mail?" Mom said to me.

"Mom, Chad, Andre, and my friend Steve have been trying very hard to get them for me. They've been to the library, H&R Block, and the post office, and there's none to be found."

"What do you mean they can't find them? I never heard of such a thing."

She continued nagging until I finally said, "Mom, what do you want me to do?" She had no concept of what it meant to ask people for a favor and then wait. This was so typical of her. Everybody jumped for her. And now she expected everyone to jump for me just to please her.

I was up all night tossing and turning, I was so upset. But my sick and insatiable need for approval caused me to continue putting up with her nonsense. I wanted to say, "Please, Mom, just leave me alone. I'm tired, I'm spent, and I'm mentally and physically burnt out from you."

I couldn't count the nights I literally crawled on my hands and knees up to my room.

About a week later Eric called to tell us that he was being transferred from D.C. to the New York office within the month. My mother and I were elated. I thought how wonderful it would be to have them so close. The other good news was they would be spending Easter with us and at that time would bring me the computer I agreed to buy from them. Lastly and most importantly, Chad had downloaded all the tax forms to Eric, and he had printed them out and would bring them Easter. To myself I said, *Thank you, God, and thank you, Chad, and thank you, Eric. Amen.*

Eric and Kim arrived the day before Easter. We all had dinner together and just hung around.

"We'll be leaving early in the morning to go into the city. We want to take a look at a few apartments. We'll be back by noon," Eric said.

He was to start work at his new firm by the middle of April.

I went to nine o'clock mass Easter Sunday. When I arrived home, I got that look from my mother, and I knew instinctively she was annoyed that it was ten thirty and Eric and Kim were still sleeping. I thought, *I have two choices here—mind my business and listen to her snide remarks or attempt to wake them up.* Either way I was doomed. The more I considered what I should do, I began to think maybe they'd appreciate my waking them up. There was that possibility they didn't realize how late it was. If it hadn't been for my mother, I'd let them sleep, and if they missed going into New York, I could care less. But once again I wanted to placate my mother just to get her off my back.

I decided to make light of it and just knock gently.

"Rise and shine," I said in a cheery tone.

Five minutes later my son came into the kitchen with a look capable of putting me six feet under.

He said something to the effect, "Why did you do that, or what's the matter with you?"

"Eric, all I did was knock one time and say rise and shine. Is that cause for your behavior now?" I said. "Grandma was getting antsy because it was getting late; you told us you were going into the city early."

What I said to myself I wouldn't even repeat. Was this the attitude I had to look forward to every visit?

I had ceased to be impressed with his Georgetown law degree; I did nothing to warrant his talking down to me. But here I was at my mother's not wanting to make a scene, so I just learned to swallow everything. This was eight and a half months of having my guts wrenched and with no letup or release. During my worst drinking days, I had never experienced anything this degrading.

I got through the afternoon serving the entire family. Everyone was gone by seven o'clock. By nine I had the entire place spic and span.

Dennis was downstairs in his comfortable little hideaway smoking.

I went into the living room and told Mom I'd read to her for a while, but not too long because I was tired. It was as though she never heard me before the words came out of her mouth.

"Listen, Roni, I want you to get a hold of Mr. Kerrigan first thing in the morning and get your forms to him so he can get my taxes done and bring them up to me," she demanded.

I sat there attempting to catch my breath and remain calm, but it was impossible.

"What do my forms have to do with your taxes?" I asked. "Mom, I am ready to drop dead right now I'm so tired, and I still came in here to read to you and you couldn't just let that subject go, could you?"

She never showed an ounce of remorse over how she upset me.

In the mail the following day were another set of tax forms Andre sent me. So now I had two complete sets of tax forms from California.

And the obedient daughter did exactly as she was told. The minute I got into work Monday morning, I called Mr. Kerrigan.

"Tell your mother not to worry; I'll bring her taxes up tonight and at the same time pick up your forms."

She still wasn't content when both of our taxes were completed and in the mail before April 15.

I knew it wouldn't be long before she started on something else. That's just the way it was and had been for eight months.

Suddenly now, she needed me to go to the bank for her twice a week. She was constantly nagging. Did I get the oil changed? Did I put gas in the car? The minute she heard the washer stop, I had to run down to put the clothes in the dryer. And again, when she heard that go off, I had to run down to fold them immediately.

There were nights I arrived home from work and would have been happy with a McDonald's hamburger, but not in my mother's home. It had to be meat and potatoes and vegetables.

Dennis was out every night, and I felt the added pressure to try to cheer her up in the evening. I would sit there at night and look at her, and my heart would break. Until she opened her mouth! Her tongue could shred me to pieces. She reminded me of Jekyll and Hyde.

The second week in April Kim and Eric moved into their new apartment in New York and he had started working at the associate firm.

Everyday the craziness got worse. Little did I know just how close we were to "The Fall of the Brennan Empire."

Out of the blue Mom asked me to go cash a check for her Wednesday. I routinely did all her banking on Saturday after my meeting.

"Are you that short on cash that you can't wait until Saturday?" I asked.

"No, I have $475 in cash," she replied. "But I still want you to go to the bank for me tomorrow."

I thought to myself that $475 cash in my pocket would be a windfall.

"Can it wait until Thursday? I asked. "I don't want to go at lunchtime and have $900 in cash in my purse. The bank is open late on Thursday, and I can go after work."

This became an ordeal because she wanted a certain amount of bills in each denomination.

"Okay," she said with an attitude.

So I obediently went to the bank after work Thursday. I cashed her check and did some grocery shopping. The bank was inside the supermarket, so why not kill two birds with one stone?

I did not feel good in work Friday, and when I got home I went right to bed. Dennis was home. I fell asleep for a short time, and when I woke, I had severe stomach cramps and went downstairs to use the bathroom.

My mother started knocking on the door, asking me in a very surly way what I was doing. From the urgency in her voice, I thought maybe she had to use the bathroom.

"Do you have to get in here?" I asked.

"No," she said nastily. Then she started yelling at me, demanding to know what was wrong with me.

"Mom, please leave me alone."

"What do you mean leave you alone? Don't I have a right to ask you what's wrong?" She was screaming.

I thought, *I've got to be in the Twilight Zone.* I could feel my blood pressure rising. No one in their right mind would believe this. When I walked out she was still standing there.

"I'm going back to bed," I said.

I was anxious to get to my meeting the following morning; it was my three-year sobriety anniversary. I had forgotten to set the alarm and overslept. The meeting was at nine. It was eight fifteen, and I was so grateful I was feeling better. I took a quick shower. By 8:40 I was ready to leave.

"Roni, can you wait until I take a shower?" she asked.

She knew I had to leave. For obvious reasons it took her quite awhile to shower and dress. That was the one thing we absolutely forbid her to do was to shower when no one was home.

"Mom, I'm already late and I'm celebrating today. Could you please wait until I get back?" I asked.

She copped an attitude, and I knew instinctively she would jump right in the shower and if anything happened it would be my fault. Dennis had already left for his meeting an hour earlier.

I was not in the best of moods when I arrived at the meeting. It was very difficult to share my experience, strength, and hope and how grateful I was to AA when my insides were doing flips and I was in the midst of all this turmoil at home. Nor was I about to divulge just how dangerous my present situation was. I had become the sacrificial lamb for this ungrateful family.

When I got home she let me know she already showered.

"Sit down, I need to talk to you," she said. "The envelope you gave me Thursday night was short $100."

I thought I was going to have a stroke; I was physically shaking. All I had done was run, run, run and jump, jump and jump higher to please her. She couldn't see across the table, but she could count her money. I went into her bedroom and counted the money, and sure enough, it was $100 short. I went through my uniform, the hamper, and my pocketbook. I went through every inch of the car.

I couldn't find the receipt from the grocery shopping I did. But I specifically remember cashing a one hundred dollar bill. But that wasn't the missing $100. Then I recalled stopping at the drugstore to pick up a prescription for her. That was accounted for, but still there was $100 missing. I know I didn't stand by the teller and count the money. There were too many bills. However, I did count it before I handed her the envelope Thursday evening, and it was the correct amount.

"I knew I should never have given into you and gone to the bank," I said.

"What's that supposed to mean?" she demanded to know.

"You didn't need that money Thursday! Now I'll be the one out $100."

Then she got nasty and asked, "Why will you be out?"

"Because I'm going to the bank right now to see if there was a mistake, and if there wasn't I'll replace that $100."

As I started to leave, she said, "Where do you think you're going?"

"To the bank," I said.

"Don't you dare walk away from me," she barked.

"Mom, Dennis is on his way here with Ashley, and I want to get back before they arrive."

Ashley is his daughter, and he was bringing her up for a visit.

She insisted I forget about the money. By now she regretted having mentioned it.

There's no way I'm going to forget about it so she can call up every one of her friends and tell them about the money I shorted her. I proceeded to leave, and she went ballistic. She was screaming hysterically and stomping her feet. Again she told me how no one cared about her and how dare I walk away from her. I was completely baffled, and she wouldn't calm down. I reached out to try to get her to sit down. She pushed me away so violently that I hit the stove and actually ended up with a quite a bruise on my arm. I was beside myself. I had watched her push me away all my life, and I swore that would be the last time she would ever do that to me again. I was so angry with myself for giving into her and going to cash that check on Thursday.

Then she started with her other routine, "I wish I would die. How would you like to be me?"

God help you, Mom, my heart has been aching for you for two whole years. I wanted to scream, *That's why I left California.*

About a half an hour later, she settled down.

"Go ahead and go to the bank," she said.

The bank had no record of an error, so I took $100 from my checking account and deposited it into her account. Not one word was ever mentioned about the money again—I never found out what happened to the $100.

When I got back I made lunch for her. Dennis and Ashley arrived around noon. He didn't have a clue what had transpired. Ashley couldn't wait to start showing me how to use the computer.

My mother was actually annoyed that Ashley was in another room with me. Teaching me how to use the computer was not going to be something that could be done in twenty minutes.

"Come on, Ashley, let's go sit with Grandma. You can come back another time and show me some more stuff."

I went up to my room for a while so Ashley could spend some time alone with her grandmother. And also so I could have a timeout from this asylum.

Next came my biggest shock of all time when out of nowhere, Dennis came up to my room and announced, "I'm picking up Drew tomorrow morning, and then we're coming back here to pick up the desk."

That was one Saturday I would never forget, the last Saturday in April.

I looked at him as though he had two heads.

Not one word had been mentioned to me that my mother had spoken to my sister-in-law, Carol during the week and all these plans were underway.

From the time I had moved there, I had no dresser or chest in my room to put my clothes in. This house with ten rooms was filled with furniture, but I didn't have a dresser. I had bought a few laundry baskets, and that's what I'd been using for nine months to store my clothes in. Heaven forbid I ask anyone to move furniture into my room. However, I was extremely grateful for the desk. At least I had all my paperwork organized and knew where everything was.

Around nine o'clock that evening, my mother announced, "You better go upstairs and empty out the desk."

"Mom, why didn't you tell me you made these arrangements?" I asked.

She just told me again to go empty it out.

I obediently went to the basement, grabbed three cardboard boxes, went up to my room, and tossed everything from the desk into the boxes. For the millionth time, I sat there and cried, looking at all my paperwork, tax returns, and letters in disarray.

Twelve years before when I was incarcerated, all I had was a cardboard box for my belongings. The more things change, the more they stay the same.

The following morning when I walked into the kitchen, Mom reminded me that Dennis and Drew were coming for the desk.

I don't know why she expected me to be there. This wasn't a social visit. Drew and my brother would be in and out within ten minutes. However, it was expected of me to be there, because my mother said so.

"Mom, I'm going to church, and I won't be back immediately afterward. I need some time alone," I said.

"What do you mean, you won't be home? Where are you going?" she asked.

"I honestly don't know," I said. "Maybe I'll just go for a walk in the park or to a movie."

Please, God, get me to church before I lose my mind, I silently pleaded.

The entire time I was in church, the one-sided conversation in my head continued. I had to keep fighting back the tears.

I wanted so much to be back in California. I wanted to be with Andre and forget I even had a mother. This woman was a foreigner to me. I didn't know who she was. I wouldn't treat a dog like she was treating me. Didn't it ever occur to her that I had a right to some privacy, a right to be tired, a right to have furniture to put my belongings in?

The past nine months had been worse than my incarceration. I spent time behind bars because of the wrongs I did. I deserved to be locked up, and I didn't have the option of walking outside the walls. But this was insane. I wasn't at my mother's for any punishment I deserved. I was there for everyone else's benefit but my own. There was no doubt that I had put myself in harm's way. This was not a place any recovering alcoholic needed to be with what little time I had in sobriety. I had just as much right to my freedom as all the other family members. I can't say I was there against my will, that's not exactly true, but surely my rights and my freedom were being denied me. Even my freedom of speech was stolen from me. *I couldn't even tell her I wouldn't be back for a lousy two hours.* She just couldn't accept that I would not jump to meet her demands. For the first time she didn't get her way, and I knew she would retaliate.

Looking back I can see that again God was watching over me. I will be eternally grateful that woman didn't push me to the brink of insanity and into the bottle.

When the service ended, I thought about my girl-friend Ellie and decided to visit her and her family. Ellie and I had been very close friends for more than thirty-five years. We had been in touch, but I hadn't seen her since I'd moved back. I had not been to her home in twenty years, and I couldn't recall where to turn off the highway. I finally gave up.

As I was driving home, I saw a sign for a motel and thought what I wouldn't give for a few hours alone in one of those rooms. It was like the car had a mind of its own, and before I even realized it, I was heading back and checking into a room. For two hours, I lay in the bed reading the Bible. I knew I had to get home, but I still wasn't ready to leave the heavenly peace and quiet of that room. I decided to go home and make dinner, and after we were done, I'd tell Mom I got a room and needed a night alone.

"Where were you all this time?" she asked. "Dennis and Drew waited and waited for you to come home."

I doubt they waited more than ten minutes. But I had disobeyed her demand, and this was just another way of laying guilt on me.

"Mom, I told you when I left this morning I wouldn't be back until later," I said.

Then she started again about how they had waited for me after they had moved the desk out.

"I didn't want to be around when they took the desk out," I said. "I didn't need it shoved in my face, what little respect I warrant around here."

I was in no mood to prolong this conversation, and I just told her I got a motel room.

"I need one night alone," I said.

She went ballistic. "What motel?"

"It really doesn't matter," I said.

I knew if I told her, she'd send Dennis to get me. Then the drama and hysterics began.

"Don't you ever think of giving any eulogy at my funeral," she screamed.

I'd already had fifty-five years of the Brennan guilt. I was not about to let her add any more to it, not after all I had done for her.

"Mom, please settle down. I just need one night alone." As I approached her to help her sit down, she shoved me away.

"You see what you just did, Mom?" I said. "You've been pushing me away all my life."

I wanted to say, *The only thing I'm any good for is serving you and entertaining you.*

I knew Dennis would be home at any minute. It was going on 5:30, and I wasn't about to listen to him. I appealed to her one more time to please understand my need to have some time alone.

"Will you be coming back here after work tomorrow?" she asked.

"Of course!"

Only in hindsight would I see the stupidity of thinking I could reason with her.

I headed directly to an AA meeting. I never felt so alone.

I spilled my guts at the meeting.

One fellow by the name of Ed came over after the meeting and knelt beside me and tried to calm me down.

I always felt better after a meeting, but much more so that evening. I could always, always, depend on the people in those meetings. I barely knew any of them, but they knew me from the Saturday morning meetings, and they certainly knew my devotion to my mother.

My stomach was in a knot all day Monday knowing I had upset her. I contemplated sending her flowers with a note telling her I was sorry. Why was I always feeling I had to justify my actions? Nothing I did pleased her.

All I so desperately wanted was some peace. I knew the things I had done in the past weren't right. And I wasn't expecting anyone to understand the reasons for my actions. But right now, I was making every attempt to change my ways and make my amends by helping at this difficult time.

I had had so much upheaval in my life in the past ten years, and I guess I had hoped that my coming to New Jersey would be beneficial to the family and, most especially, my mother. I knew it would never be a happily ever after situation. I just wanted things to be fair and to be shown the respect I deserved for my efforts.

AA taught me how to live one day at a time. I had learned to trust God. I could not tolerate the daily confrontations. My job was very demanding, yet I looked forward to those few hours away from my mother. The pressure of the job was nothing compared to the constant stress and tension of trying to please her.

When five o'clock rolled around, all I wanted to do was get home and face the music, make my apologies, and try a little harder. I knew she would be a nervous wreck if I was not home by 5:20. I was terribly eager for this day to be over.

I pulled in the driveway and was barely out of the car when Dennis came storming out of the house and demanded I give him the keys, "Now!" The Pavlovian reflex took over, and I just handed them to him. Not in a billion years would I have ever believed I'd hear the words.

"Mom wants you out of here!" he said.

I felt an icy chill and wanted to crumble to the ground and just stay there.

"This can't possibly be over my going to a motel for one night," I said.

I thought back to the day we discussed his moving in and how I specified that, if there were any problems, I was not going to be the one to move out.

Homelessness, my worst fear, was now my reality. My mother knew exactly where to strike to hurt me the most.

"Can I keep the car for a few days?" I asked.

"No!"

"Would you drive me to a motel?"

"No!"

Four cars in the driveway and only one person with a license, yet they wouldn't allow me to keep one for a few days.

I stood there watching Dennis holding on to those keys for dear life. The locksmith was on his way to change the locks. It was so symbolic of how they thought they could control everything.

I was the one who had a past, and, as an ex-offender, my life was now divided into before and after. I was the daughter who had been there for her every day for the past year, and, in one selfish, angry moment, she now thrust the knife that would cleave my heart in two.

Most families could forgive a daughter who had struggled against all the odds to turn her life around, but not my family. They could only identify with the worst that I had done. They never even asked why I was incarcerated. Not one of them cared enough to inquire as to what led to my arrest.

They couldn't remember nine months prior when I stayed up around the clock to care for my dad, and nine months before that taking a leave of absence and coming to New Jersey to care for Patrick. She couldn't remember who drove home on her lunch hour every day for six weeks and took her for radiation treatments, while Dennis did nothing. He wasn't even working.

My mother would turn my decision to go to a motel for one night into the most vicious act, committed with the sole intent to upset her. It was always about her.

My mother was like a magnet, forcefully pulling me in her direction. I was so afraid of losing the love I never had. I had dropped everything to run to her. I had rearranged my life to accommodate her, and she had done nothing but use me, and now she was discarding me. I felt violated in a way not even prison had made me feel.

BANISHED AND
HOMELESS *AGAIN*

"Roni, you need to get some help," were Dennis's last words.

This dismissal, in my mind, was like throwing a non-swimmer overboard in the middle of the ocean and yelling, "You need to go for swimming lessons!" I was being kicked out in the street with no place to go and no car to get there, he wouldn't even drive me to a motel, yet he was yelling at me to go for help. Now I was the mad daughter and sister.

I had his permission to use the phone.

"Hi, Katie, could you please give me a ride to a motel?" I asked. "I'll explain later."

"Sure. I'll be over in a few minutes."

When she arrived, she helped me pack a few things. I was visibly shaking. I just wanted to get away from there. We threw a few things in a brown paper bag and took off.

After getting settled in the motel room, I called Eric at work and told him what had happened. This was *my* son, the attorney, who recently moved to New York with his wife. I was aghast to learn he knew all about it.

"Grandma is absolutely beside herself," he said. "She doesn't want you living there anymore."

"Dennis refused to drive me to a motel," I said.

"I'm glad to hear you're okay," he told me.

I thought, *What a strange thing to say!* By his remark, it was obvious there was a concern that maybe I wouldn't be able to handle this banishment very well. But clearly, he hadn't cared enough to call me at work and forewarn me.

I related the events of the weekend to him, but I could tell from his silence he had already chosen sides, and it was *not* his mother's. He wouldn't even offer to lend me his car that was being stored at my mother's, the third unused car in her driveway.

I asked him if I could come over and spend the weekend with them.

"Kim is very angry with you," he said.

"What's Kim got to be angry about?" I asked.

"Is it true that you yelled at your mother?" he asked.

"Eric, you know better than anyone that I have never in my life yelled at my mother."

Lies, rumors, innuendos, and tea leaves, that's what my fate now rested in.

Echoing in the recesses of my mind were St. Augustine's words, "Heal me of this lust of mine to always vindicate myself." Even knowing I had done the best I could, it was a habit borne of a lifetime of guilt and accusations. Today, my mother had lain to rest any thought that maybe things had changed and she did love me.

How does one stop vindicating oneself when one is so desperate for approval?

Here was an eighty-five-year-old woman who was nearly blind and had recently experienced two very traumatic losses along with her own illness. Yet, within an eight-hour period, she had the presence of mind to pull off a very methodical plan.

She got Kim to drop everything and take a bus from New York to New Jersey to get their car out of the driveway before I came "home." No, not home, that was a Freudian slip.

She had managed to convince my brothers that I deserved to be kicked out. She had called my son Chad in California to say the same thing. She had called Eric at his office. Lastly, she had convinced my sister-in-law that she needed her home for protection for a few hours and had my daughter-in-law whisk her away to safety before I returned from work.

Her timing was exquisite. My son had moved to New York one month prior, and now she had seen to it that I would never enjoy his company again. By her own admission, she was jealous of my relationship with my sons and their successes.

My family had ambushed me with the element of surprise, most successfully.

We talk in AA about alcohol being cunning, baffling, and powerful. My mother was right up there with one of the most destructive forces I had ever known. She too was cunning, baffling, and powerful, but not until that day did I realize her extreme hatred of me.

An hour later, Katie came back with coffee, and we went to a meeting.

The PA system in my head was in full swing when I got in bed. I wanted to crawl under the blankets and then have someone wake me up and tell me Mom had made a mistake and she was sorry and wanted me to come home. I knew I could not face going into work the following morning. Yet I could not afford to take the day off, and mentally I could not afford the luxury of feeling sorry for myself. I dreaded going to sleep.

> I will lie down and sleep; I wake again, because the Lord sustains me.
>
> Psalm 3:5 (NIV)

It was not yet five o'clock when I climbed out of bed exhausted. I ran to the pay phone to call ahead for a cab. My stomach was in a knot thinking about going into work. Mom had a talent for beguiling people with her poor little innocent veneer. Who would believe me when I said I hadn't done anything to cause this? My world had been shaken again. The overriding shame and humiliation already had me in a choke hold.

I walked to the motel's restaurant and bought a cup of coffee, and then stood on the balcony watching the sun come up and listening to the birds twittering away. I returned to the room and read my devotionals. I closed my eyes and prayed. Then I picked up the Bible and started reading.

Arriving at my job, I immediately plunged into the pile of work on my desk. Laura, the lab technician, and

I were the only two who worked on the second floor. Mornings were her busiest time, so we seldom saw one another before ten thirty. I had a steady stream of patients coming in for referrals.

Around eleven o'clock, she came in to make a copy of a lab report. We exchanged our usual greetings.

"How did things go when you got home yesterday?" she asked.

"Mom kicked me out!" I said. "I'm back at the motel right now. In fact, I almost called you for a ride this morning, but I didn't have your phone number." It was buried under all the rubble in my *used-to-be* bedroom.

She had an incredulous look on her face.

"Roni, I can't believe it. Not after all you did for Patrick and your father," she said. Her face showed true compassion.

"Would you like to go out for lunch?" she asked.

"Definitely," I said.

Sharon was on her way up to the coffee room and stuck her head in the door.

"How's everything going?" she asked.

I told her what had happened.

"What! But why?"

"That's the $64,000 question," I said.

She agreed to join us for lunch.

I called a rental agency and arranged to pick up a car at lunch time. Then I drove to the restaurant.

I explained what had happened and how Dennis had demanded I give him the keys and told me, "Mom wants you out of the house," but he wouldn't give me a reason. We dissected every event of the weekend and concluded nothing could justify anything this radical.

When we returned to the office, I called my brother Todd. I hoped he had the good sense to know I didn't deserve this. Wrong! He had already spoken to Mom, and together they had chewed me up and spit me out.

"Todd, can you give me some explanation for Mom doing this to me?" I asked.

I will never forget his exact words.

"I think it's you who needs to do some explaining to me," he demanded pointedly.

Had my father still been alive, I would have sworn he was on the other end with the immediate assertion of power and control that I hated so much.

This wasn't supposed to happen. I needed to ask the questions. Again, the conditioned response had me rehearsing every detail of the weekend. Why did I always end up with the saddle on my back with the horse riding me?

"Well, I don't know what to believe," he said. "I wasn't there."

"I hope this isn't going to cause a repeat of our past estrangement," I said.

When he remained silent, I had my answer, which only served to magnify my anguish.

"Good-bye, Roni."

How could any of them doubt how much I cared? How could they believe her lies?

I was lost in my reverie until a few girls came up to talk to me and asked if there was anything they could do. Their concern was very comforting.

It was an extremely busy afternoon. I couldn't believe when I looked up and saw it was already five o'clock. I was so glad to have a car to drive back to the motel.

I went to a meeting that evening, and a fellow gave me the name and phone number of a friend who was a car salesman. I called him the following morning, and by ten o'clock that evening, I had a car. By the following morning, it was insured. By noontime, the rental was returned.

From a woman's standpoint, the only thing I knew for sure was the interior and exterior were in perfect condition. It had four brand new tires, and the price was right. I had no way of knowing how trustworthy this fellow was, but I had no doubt God had led me to him, and that was enough for me.

> Unless the Lord had given me help, I would soon
> have dwelt in the silence of death.
>
> Psalm 94:17(NIV)

With great trepidation, I tried to reach my mother to see if I could stop by to get some of my belongings. Her line had been busy all day. At seven o'clock, I finally reached her.

"You can stop by later," she said. "Dennis is at a meeting and will be home at nine thirty."

"Thanks."

I was so nervous talking to her, but still I thought she would regret her hastiness and, no doubt, would tell me to come home. Stupid me! She had no lingering regrets. Whatever made me move back and fall prey to her sheer loathing of me? Who was this stranger whom I had taken care of for nine months? When I lived with her, I had to remain home every night. Now, suddenly, it was okay for her to be "home alone."

When I arrived, Dennis let me in. Glancing in my mother's direction, where she sat in her usual cane-back chair, all I saw was hatred etched on her face. She never said one word to me. I went to the basement for a few empty boxes. Suddenly, Dennis erupted and started screaming, "You're not coming in here at this hour and packing stuff up." He followed me up to the bedroom and watched every move I made.

"Dennis, I haven't even been here ten minutes," I said. "Mom instructed me to come at this time."

This wasn't a battle, this was a full-fledged war, and I had no fight left in me. I held back the words that were on the tip of my tongue. In times of crisis, which this obviously was, there comes an enduring strength and consolation from above.

> He that is slow to wrath is of great understanding,
> but he that is hasty of spirit displays folly.
>
> Proverbs 14:29 (NIV)

There was a sense of spiritual satisfaction by keeping silent. Still, I wanted to cry staring at the contents of the cardboard boxes strewn all over the floor and the laundry baskets with all my clothes in them. She wasn't happy taking what I thought was my home away and the car; now she didn't even want me to have my clothes. My blood boiled when I thought of Andre shipping eighteen boxes of my belongings back here.

I could barely hold on to the clothes that were clasped in my arms, my body was trembling so badly. As I walked past her, my insides wanted to scream, "Mom, I can't be perfect for you right now. I'm sorry, I'm sorry. Whatever I did wrong, I'm sorry. Please stop hurting me." I stumbled into the car. I drove without seeing. I walked without feeling, and I fell into bed with an overwhelming fear of waking up.

I did wake! I immediately thought back to the night before. How pathetic to see Dennis playing the role of Mom's bodyguard! It wouldn't take long before he realized he was on the same sinking ship; all he had done was change seats with me. She used him to kick me out, and she would continue to use him. I just could not understand Dennis's volatile behavior.

Robert Frost said, "Home is the one place we can return to where they have to take you in."

I was still living in that fantasy, believing I could return and be accepted. How I envied those who could return home and kick off their shoes, get comfortable, and be silly without being criticized or judged.

I grudgingly thanked God for my freedom, as painful as that freedom was right now, and I thanked him from the depths of my soul for my job.

Even with all the anguish and uncertainty, I felt a new kind of peace. The Lord had me right where I needed to be. I had nothing and no one to turn to, but I trusted him to help me begin over.

The busyness of the office became my saving grace when my mind's replay button seemed to be stuck. A few patients would come in and occupy an hour of my time, and then, without warning, I'd be zoned out and feeling sorry for myself.

The phone would bring me back to reality, but the minute I hung up, I'd be staring out the window and praying not to break down. The thought of losing my composure and not being able to come back to any semblance of sanity terrified me. I could not afford that luxury right now, and if I did, who would I turn to for help? The family I loved had abandoned me.

Laura, Sharon, and I had lunch together in my office. I told them what happened the night before. They were shocked at Dennis's behavior.

If I hadn't intervened on his behalf, I would still have a place to go home to. I had been genuinely concerned for Dennis when his wife left him. I had taken him to meetings, provided a sympathetic ear, encouraged him, and given him hope that things would get better.

I recalled a story the pastor had told a few years back:

It was a very cold day, but also very beautiful. Snoopy noticed the frozen lake, ran down, jumped on it, and started gliding and sliding all over the icy lake. He was having so much fun. Along comes Lucy.

"What are you doing?" she asks.

"I'm skating," Snoopy says.

"You're so dumb; you can't skate," Lucy says.

Snoopy ignores her and continues skating, and he's having a blast. Lucy yells again.

"You're so stupid, dogs can't skate."

Snoopy starts thinking about what Lucy said and he stopped, went over, and sat down on a log.

"Gee, I thought I was having a great time," read the caption above his head.

Gee, Mom, I thought I was doing such a good job. There had been no warning signs, not a clue that Mom was so dissatisfied. The cruelty of those words, "Mom doesn't want you here anymore," would haunt me for the rest of my life. My spirit had, indeed, been crushed.

One minute I was excited about the car, and the next I was lying in a motel room depressed, reliving the past few months. It was time to read the Word again.

> I will lie down and sleep in peace, for you alone, O Lord, make me dwell in safety.
>
> Psalm 4:8 (NIV)

I could not return to that depressing motel room when I got out of work. I stopped at McDonald's to get a bite to eat. Having read about the Thursday evening Life Group in the church bulletin, I decided that it would be wise at this time to join them.

I immediately felt at home when I arrived. What a strange thought, at the same time, a pleasant concept.

Ten people, eight of whom I had never met before, were conversing about Jesus as though he were one of us. They asked questions about things that never crossed my mind. They were courteous and hospitable.

What would they think if they knew about my past? I just wanted to spill my guts and tell them I was a homeless person. I wanted to tell them about a mother who had kicked her daughter out into the street. No, not yet! That would be too much information, leading to way too many questions.

"Being a Christian is very hard," Cathy said to the group.

Denise agreed, "It's been quite a struggle for Kevin and me to overcome our drug addiction."

I almost fell off the chair. Kevin was the assistant pastor, and Denise was his wife. We were, at that moment, in their home. That evening opened a whole new universe to me. My mind could never conceive of church people struggling with addictions. Denise and Kevin had recently moved to New Jersey from California, which immediately gave us something in common.

"I need to ask a question," I said. "My mother recently did something that has caused me a great deal of anguish. I don't want to hate her, but I can't seem to help it. I'm really struggling. Is there any insight you can give me?"

"Roni, that's the devil," Cecile said. "He's always tugging at us to do wrong. His whole purpose is to get us to hate."

The discussion continued back and forth for the next two hours and ended when we formed a circle and a few people prayed aloud. I had never been exposed to this type of service, so I remained silent. They served cake and coffee, and we hung around chatting for about a half hour.

My mind was racing when I left there. What a wonderful experience: to express my opinion freely and not be criticized, to ask a question and have it answered in a courteous manner. The ability to remain silent and the willingness to listen to Cecile's suggestion graciously was an indication something supernatural was stirring in me. The ideology of the enemy had not been something I wanted to learn about, but that night it all made sense.

Sir Thomas Moore declared:

> Knowing that I knew nothing, I had the heart to believe that what my ignorance concealed from me was not terrible, but finer than anything so far discovered, and I dared push forward into all truth. For, suspecting that my light was in reality but shadow, I was confident that beyond the shadow I would find God.

I knew my ignorance was not terrible because now I had a new adventure into which I could enter, while searching for God's truth and peace. I would be there the following Thursday and every Thursday after that.

I had called my mother earlier to get permission to pick up a few more things. She was home alone, so I had to wait until nine thirty. Dennis let me in, and I encountered the same freeze. I quickly grabbed what I absolutely needed and left. Dennis helped me out, but only because he had an ulterior motive.

"Is that your car?" he asked.

"Yes!"

"Mom told me you were complaining about me going out every night to meetings and leaving you to clean up after dinner."

"No, Dennis, I never complained about cleaning up or you going out. I complained about your smoking in the basement every minute you were home. You had made a promise before you moved in that you would not smoke in the house. Stop trying to involve me in an argument you're having with yourself. I'm not up it to right now."

I realized he resented having to go back into the house while I had the freedom to drive away. Without me there, he was left to face the truth of his misery, and it had nothing to do with me. He had gotten what he wanted, a nice place to live, free rent and utilities, plus food and the freedom to come and go as he pleased, and he didn't have to work. But his buffer was gone, and now he was left alone with "Mommy Dearest."

I called in sick the following morning. Everyone in the office understood it had been a very trying week.

The women's AA meeting I occasionally attended was having a celebration party that evening. I had told my sponsor I would meet her there early to set up the tables.

The speaker, the food, the fellowship, and the laughter made it the perfect evening. After we cleaned up, we took all the helium balloons outside. Each balloon represented a problem we had. We released them and watched them go up to God, knowing he would give each one his special attention. I slept very peacefully that night.

Sunday morning, I went to church, and I know God intended for me to hear this particular sermon: "Life Isn't Fair." The timing was crucial because following the service, I was going to my mother's to meet my son so that he could help pack up my belongings. The message was the catalyst that began the process of relinquishing my anger and hurt before I arrived.

I can't recall everything the pastor said, but just those three words reverberated in my head and applied to exactly what I was going through at the time.

He gave several examples of things that had happened to people that weren't fair. The more I thought about it, the more I realized it was just that simple. It wasn't fair. There were people who survived worse situations by trusting the Lord. They moved beyond their individual situation and in the end came out ahead. Everything hinged on letting God help me get through this.

When we were done, Eric and I sat for about an hour and chatted. Or more like I talked and he listened.

"Eric, my mother is a very bitter and angry person. She lost her security and the son she worshipped."

Her entire world revolved around Patrick. For years, my dad had wanted to move to Florida, and they had discussed it many times. But they had decided against it because Mom couldn't leave Patrick. They stayed in New Jersey and kept the house because it provided a place for Patrick to come on his days and weekends off.

"She expected me to be her eyes, her husband, and her son. She couldn't accept me for just being me. I have stood in Patrick's shadow my entire life, and I had no problem with that until now," I told him.

Transference! She was transferring her anger to me because she knew I was the only person who wouldn't strike back.

A few minutes later, my daughter-in-law came into the room to remind Eric they had to leave shortly for an appointment. They were taking Mom to look at an assisted living home.

"No matter what my mother did, I could never stop loving her."

"You should tell her that, but not until you can do it without crying."

First, I'm badgered with accusations, now its stipulations. I can't even cry. Wow!

But a few minutes later, I did it.

This situation was still so present that I could never have foreseen just how far and how long these repercussions would continue.

In regards to my son and his wife, I wasn't taking any of this personally. I was sure it would blow over.

Meanwhile, Eric wasn't about to disagree with his wife in defense of his mother. I was the mother-in-law who had a past, had a drinking problem, and suddenly I was now mentioning the word God. And that definitely put me in the weird category of people you don't want to be associated with. They had moved up to the west side; they were in the big league.

"Mom, I'm sorry for whatever I did to bring this separation about." I leaned over and kissed her and said, "I love you."

She sat there completely stoic, as if her behavior was justified. There's a saying we use in recovery which is, "keeping our side of the street clean." Although I knew in my heart and soul that I had done nothing to warrant the outcome of her actions, I had to say those few words to her, just to give me some peace of mind.

From the day I set foot in New Jersey, I swore I would never allow myself to fall into any verbal confrontations. I did not want the emotional hangover that comes from words said in anger. At the same time, I knew I had allowed this to go on for far too long. Now it was too late, and added to my anguish, I had to come face to face with her indifference and complete lack of caring as to how this was affecting me.

She sat there not attempting to say one word to me, nothing to comfort me, or give me any hint that she had some regrets. It was as if she didn't even want to acknowledge my existence. She was nothing more than the host who had carried me inside her womb; together, she and my father had given me life. Then they spent the next fifty-five years destroying it.

I had lost my father, my brother, and she had now brought about this estrangement with my remaining two brothers, my son, my daughter-in-law, and my niece and nephews. And, because I cared too much, I had ended a nine-year relationship to move back to New Jersey to help my family. Ninety-five percent of what I owned had been given away, four percent was in storage three thousand miles away, and the remaining one percent I now had to beg for and carry alone into a motel room.

For the next three hours, I lay in bed and tormented myself.

Regardless of one's age, betrayal and rejection are severe and bitter. There were times I thought I had fallen down the same hole Alice had. Nothing could have been more bizarre than this.

Why did I always wait till I was in so much pain before I reached for his Word?

> Do not let this Book of the Law depart from your mouth; meditate on it day and night, so that you may be careful to do everything written in it.
>
> Joshua 1:8 (NIV)

BLESSED WITH *MY* NEW CAR AND *MY* NEW APARTMENT

Sunday evening, I went to the same AA meeting I had been at the week before. It was a room full of strangers, a few acquaintances, none of whom I had to cook or clean for, yet they showed more concern for me than my own family did. They had helped me find a car, had taken me to a meeting, and were willing to do whatever they could to get me through this.

"Roni, why don't you look in the newspaper for an apartment listed by a realtor?" Gail suggested.

"I never thought of that," I said. "To be honest, I wasn't aware that people listed apartment rentals with realtors."

"Oh, sure, my cousin went through a realtor. They have a complete listing and can accommodate your specific requirements."

On the way back to the motel, I picked up a paper. I circled some ads that looked good. The following morning, I called and made an appointment with a realtor for seven o'clock that evening.

After work, I went back to the motel and lay down. I was depressed just thinking about going to look at apartments. I called to cancel but the line was busy. I forced myself to get up; it was better than staying in the room.

> But those who hope in the Lord will renew their strength. They will soar on wings like eagles; they will run and not grow weary, they will walk and not be faint.
>
> Psalm 40:31 (NIV)

The first place we went to look at was great, but the owner insisted on a credit check.

"To be honest, my credit is not the best," I said. "I have a very good job and would be willing to give an extra month's security, if that would help."

"No, we've had too many problems in the past."

The realtor mentioned a two-family with a basement apartment that was available. She called the owners, and they invited us right over.

I wanted to beg off and go back to the motel room. It was close to ten o'clock, and I knew this would be a waste of time.

When we arrived, a young couple showed us in. The apartment had a huge bedroom with a full bath, a big living room with a dining area; the kitchen was a good size with all new cabinets. There was another small office off the kitchen. We agreed to meet after work the following day to sign the papers. I was ecstatic. I held my breath for the next eighteen hours; this was too good to be true.

The next day, I asked, "Sharon, how would you like to take a ride with me after work to see the apartment?"

I needed her support.

"Sure. I'll follow you."

Sherry and P.J., the landlords, had the lease all prepared. The realtor had already arrived. Sharon and I took a quick glance through, and I signed the papers and gave them a check. The apartment was mine. Sharon stood there in awe.

"Roni, this place is fantastic!"

"I've never had an apartment this big. I can't believe it's mine."

I drove back to the motel and packed a few things.

It was after ten o'clock when I arrived back at the apartment. My adrenaline was pumping as I walked through the door. Being there alone and having the time to look around slowly and take it all in was exhilarating. The entire apartment sparkled. It had just been painted. The carpeting was in perfect condition.

The probability of getting a car and an apartment in seven days, under my circumstances, seemed far less than my chances of winning the lottery.

The only thing I owned was the computer I had bought from my son. In this apartment was one piece of furniture: a computer desk.

"Sherry, did the previous tenant leave that desk?"

"No, it's mine, but I have no use for it. You can have it."

Sherry had no clue what was going on in my mind. And no words could adequately convey my excitement at that moment. I wanted to shout, "Wow!"

Sharon told the girls at work about *my* awesome apartment. She had brought me towels and sheets and a quilt. She also gave me an electric coffeepot and mugs.

I felt like a little kid at Christmas driving home and thinking about going into *my* new home. I walked through the door and just stood there savoring the view. This performance called for an encore many more times.

My kitchen, with an oven and a refrigerator! I had stopped at the grocery store and bought eggs and milk and a few other basics. I had towels, sheets, and a blanket to sleep on. I had a coffeepot and mugs. I didn't care if I had to sleep on the floor forever.

Every day was like having a bridal shower. The girls from the office kept bringing in more stuff for me. One girl gave me a set of glasses and a blender. Another one gave me a little television and a portable phone. Another one gave me a set of dishes and silverware. I had my Walkman and a bunch of cassettes. I could get up in the morning, have my coffee, read my devotionals, and do my exercises.

One day at a time, the same principle Jesus taught us in "The Lord's Prayer." *Give us this day, our daily bread. Thank you, Lord, you knew exactly what I needed each day, and you provided me with each of those needs.* In time, I would learn to hold everything with an open hand. God had been very good to me. There would be no need to clutch or grab anything ever again.

The one who loved to debate everything people said was finally learning the virtue of silence.

> Let all the earth be silent before him. Lord, I have heard of your fame; I stand in awe of your deeds, O Lord.
>
> Habakkuk 2:20, 3:2 (NIV)

Two weeks passed by quickly. I read in the church bulletin that there was a trip on Saturday for the women. They were going to visit an associate church. It listed the itinerary for the day, and it sounded like a lot of fun.

Eric called me on Wednesday.

"Hi, Mom, how are you doing?" "I'm fine. How are you doing?"

"Good. I spoke to Grandma last night, and she said you could have the single bed."

"Oh! That's great!"

"Dennis and I will bring it over Saturday."

"I won't be home, but I'll leave the key under the mat. Thanks for taking care of this for me."

My apartment was only ten minutes from my mother's. I gave Eric the directions. I was very happy about this. I had absolutely no furniture in the apartment.

I had been counting the hours for a week now. I was so excited about going on this trip. Still, the need for quiet time forced me to flee to the rear of the bus. Images of past bus trips where I was in shackles, wearing state-issued clothes, and surrounded by guards flashed through my mind. How different to be on this bus with the precious gift of freedom, wearing a white peasant dress, traveling to a beautiful church on the Delaware Water Gap, and surrounded by Christian women.

I had no clue where we were going or the purpose of this trip.

"Veronika, go with the flow," he whispered silently.

"Thank you, Lord."

It was a mystery tour with no expectations and no preconceived notions. What a strange phenomenon, this unexplainable joy. I was free, free, free! This was not a dream; this was freedom from every responsibility. I could throw my watch out the window for a day. No tugging, no one pulling, no criticisms, no judgments, and no one making demands on my time. Wow!

When the bus pulled into the parking lot, I was the last one to get off as I nervously followed the women into a beautiful church auditorium.

Had I blinked my eyes and clicked my heels twice, I would have thought I had been magically transported inside a marvelous farm house at harvest time. There were haystacks and barrels overflowing with apples.

Everywhere I turned, I saw an array of handmade arts and crafts. There were partitions and backdrops giving the appearance of individual rooms. One area was a country kitchen with gingham curtains hanging on the windows, and the walls were lined with an assortment of canning jars filled with jams and fruits. Another area was an old-fashioned sewing room with bales of material on the shelves. There was a porch with rocking chairs.

I needed an invisible friend to reach up and shut my mouth; it seemed as though I was doing a lot of gaping.

I saw multicolored mums and flowers brimming from the most beautiful pottery jars. There were baskets full of little cupcakes, tea biscuits, corn bread, fruits, and juices for us to choose from.

A few hours later, we assembled in the main hall, where a wonderful luncheon had been prepared, and I was served a little taste of contentment with a topping of heaven.

"As we face the uncertainty of the new millennium, we are reminded of the importance of what is meant by *discernment*. Yes, we are to trust God for everything and in everything. But that does not mean we are to be careless or reckless by not making some preparations for what we might face at midnight this upcoming New Year's Eve. We are not to say, 'Oh well, even if we are left without water or electricity, God will take care of it.' We are to do our part and prepare for the possibility we may be left without water and electricity. Again, that does not mean that we are to run to Costco and buy every case of water on the shelf."

The speaker continued to elaborate on what our part was and what God's part was, using the New Year's Eve threat as an illustration. That lecture still stands as the single greatest example of what *discernment* means and how it affects the decisions I make in my spiritual walk with the Lord.

If I had one wish, it would be the ability to develop the cinematic pictures my mind had captured that day. On the ride home, we sang songs of praise and worship. I can still remember a few words from one song because it described what the Lord had done for me that day. *He picked me up from the miry clay.*

> He put a new song in my mouth, a hymn of praise to our God.
>
> Psalm 40:3 (NIV)

We arrived back at the church parking lot around seven o'clock. I drove to my mother's to pick up a few more things and to see Eric. He and Dennis had taken my mother out to dinner. Eric gave me a bouquet of flowers for Mother's Day, which was the following day. He had also given my mother a bouquet. I only stayed for a short time. I thanked my mother for the bed, and then I left.

It would have been a wonderful end to a perfect day had Eric suggested we spend Sunday together and offered to take me out to dinner. His wife was out of town for a few days. Had he forgotten I was *his* mother?

A knot the size of California was in my stomach.

> Since you have never been this way before, keep a distance. The Lord will do amazing things among you.
>
> Joshua 4:5 (NIV)

As soon as I arrived home, I made the bed. The simple pleasures in life! A mattress to sleep on! The wonder of being able to call this place, *Home Sweet Home!* And the miracle of knowing the sincerity of the words I uttered in silence, *Thank you, Lord.*

Sunday, I went to church. Later that afternoon, I made my own special Mother's Day dinner and invited the Lord to join me. I would never be alone again.

Chad called from California to wish me a Happy Mother's Day, and we had a nice chat.

> May the Lord grant you … a home in which you will find rest.
>
> Ruth 1:9 (NIV)

TRIPLE BLESSINGS: LIFE GROUP, AUNT BETTY, AND STEVE

Thursday evening I went to the Life Group and was pleasantly surprised to find out this was *fun* night.

I needed some fun after the week I had had. The night before, I had stopped by my mom's after work to drop off a brochure about a nearby assisted living facility. As I was sliding it under the door, Dennis saw me. I told him what it was.

"Wait a minute," he said.

He asked my mother if she wanted to talk to me. I was then given permission to come in for a minute.

"How are you doing?" she asked.

"Mom, I'm crushed," I said.

"Well, it hasn't been easy for me," she responded.

She had kicked me out, and now it was all about how it was affecting her. I wanted to scream, *You couldn't even begin to fathom the depth of my pain. You have caused me more anguish and heartache than I will ever permit anyone to know.*

I left immediately, regretting having gone there. I was determined not to allow my mother to ruin another one of my evenings.

At Life Group, there were ten people of varying ages, sizes, shapes, and colors, all happy to see me arrive.

Denise and Kevin were busy barbequing the hamburgers and hot dogs. Everyone had brought a special dish, along with rolls and drinks. There was no cause to fret about arriving empty-handed.

Afterward, we played "Charades" and "Gestures." I can still remember one high school student stomping around the kitchen pretending to be a dinosaur, as he acted out *Jurassic Park.* We laughed hysterically.

A time to weep and a time to laugh.

Ecclesiastes 3:4 (NIV)

Simplicity and kindness, no pride or arrogance, no pointing fingers, just one evening of fun and games with the knowledge that God was on the sidelines rooting for me as I attempted to pantomime a bumblebee so my teammates would guess *The Sting.* It could have been worse; imagine having to act out *Butch Cassidy and the Sundance Kid!*

This was an unknown world to me. Had anyone guessed what was going on in my mind, surely they would have thought I'd spent the last twenty years in a cave.

As the evening drew to a close, we all joined hands and prayed.

I was just about to leave when something prompted me to speak up. Another new experience for me!

"Does anybody know where I could get some furniture?" I asked. "I just moved into my own apartment, and I don't have any."

"I sure do," George said. "I have a dresser and chest for the bedroom and a sofa and chair for the living room, and I'm not using any of it."

"I have a truck. We can load it up next Friday night and bring it over," Tom said.

I was ecstatic as I stood there with my mouth hanging open again! I mentioned needing furniture. Voilà! My apartment was now furnished.

Ten minutes later, behind the wheel, all alone in my car, I burst into laughter, knowing there would be no more humming, "*De-De, De-De, De-De, De-De,*" the tune to *The Twilight Zone*. The flood of tears quickly followed, as I cried out, "Lord, please forgive me for all the years I ignored you." I knew I had hurt myself with all my wrongdoing, but that evening, I knew it was nothing compared to how much I had hurt him.

The following Friday, Tom and George delivered the furniture as promised, along with a cabinet for my little television.

"George, let me give you something for all this," I said.

"No way! I'm glad you can use it."

By nine o'clock the following morning, my "new" used furniture was in its proper place. My clothes were all in drawers, no more laundry baskets, and I knew I would never again have to store my belongings in a cardboard box.

This had been one of those rare moments when I understood exactly what Jesus meant. I was not experiencing a childish immaturity; I was feeling a childlike happiness that was so new to me and so wonderful! The first time I ever felt that way was when I was with my Aunt Betty and her daughter, Kathy.

"Yoo-hoo! My name is Helen," my mother said. "Do you mind if I walk with you? I see the two of you on the bus every day."

"Sure, you can join us. I'm Betty, and this is my sister, Rita."

So began a deep and abiding friendship among the three women that continued for sixty-plus years.

After I was born, Betty became my godmother. Sixty years later, I still call her Aunt Betty. In secret, I refer to her as my guardian angel. Jim, her husband, became Uncle Jimmy. He was the fun-loving, handsome, and robust love of her life. He also was the one who could magically turn our family's boring parties into happy occasions when he began with his jokes and storytelling.

Just the mention of their names triggers memories of the big colonial house, the familiar smells of homemade apple pie, and the welcoming hugs Aunt Betty and Uncle Jimmy always gave me. I still have pictures of all the birthday parties for their daughter, Kathy, along with the birthday parties at our home.

When I turned twenty-two, I sat in the sunporch under a beautiful frilly shower umbrella, opening bridal presents in that big colonial house. The years had flown by, but Aunt Betty and Uncle Jimmy were still the special couple who shared in the excitement of my upcoming marriage.

"Oh, Roni, we're truly thrilled for you," said Aunt Betty. "Brad is so handsome."

A few years later, their daughter, Kathy, became engaged. Uncle Jimmy passed away before Kathy and her fiancé, Ken, were married.

Every year, Aunt Betty sent me a birthday card. When we moved to California she continued sending cards and wrote to me often. Every Christmas, she sent me pictures of her two grandchildren.

Her sincere interest in everything we did and her encouraging words always warmed by heart. "We miss you, but I talk to your mom every week, and she keeps me updated. I'm amazed at all you've accomplished in such a short time. I hear you're back in college nights. You should be very proud of yourself. I know I am."

Whenever I came back to visit, she always made it a point to have me over. We chatted for hours, letting nothing else come between our conversations.

Kathy, her daughter, is a registered nurse, who is very much like her mother. When I moved back to New Jersey, they both made me feel like I was the only person on earth.

Aunt Betty would start by telling me about the times Chad and Eric had visited. "They're the nicest boys and so good-looking. Roni, you must be genuinely proud of them."

Our conversations were always upbeat and cheerful. Aunt Betty knew about my past but never mentioned it. I could be in her company *sans* the mask and for those few hours just be myself and know she loved me.

Do not judge, or you too will be judged.

Matthew 7:1 (NIV)

The week my mother did her banishing act, Aunt Betty was in the hospital recuperating from hip surgery. After church on Sunday, I drove to the bakery and picked up some crumb buns and jelly doughnuts. From there, I went to Kathy's, and together we drove to the hospital. Aunt Betty was feeling pretty well despite her discomfort. She was an amazing woman who had experienced more than her share of medical problems.

"Hi, Aunt Betty. I'm so sorry you had to go through this," I said.

"Oh well, what are you going to do?" she replied.

When she said that, I realized what made her so special.

"I'll be fine," she said and immediately asked about me. "Tell me, Roni, about you. How you are doing?" The sadness in her eyes had nothing to do with *her* pain. I could read her thoughts and feel her empathy. *Oh, Roni, I wish I could do something for you.*

"I had hoped that by now you and your mom would have worked out your differences," Aunt Betty said.

"Mom won't even talk to me."

"I spoke to your mom a few days ago, but she never said a word about it. Kathy told me."

My mother was shrewd enough to know she could never convince Aunt Betty I had done anything to deserve the severity of her wrath. Aunt Betty was not a person who would judge me on innuendos and false accusations. She knew how hard I tried to please my mother.

As we visited and ate our jelly doughnuts, Aunt Betty once again turned the topic to my concerns, not hers. Aunt Betty was the patient, yet she was the balm that soothed me that day.

> I am concerned for you and will look on you with favor.
>
> Ezekiel 36:9 (NIV)

After we left the hospital, Kathy and I went out for dinner.

"Kathy, I just wish someone would tell me what I did to bring this about. It's the not knowing that will be my undoing."

Kathy had played an integral part in helping my family during these difficult months. She had witnessed my efforts to care for Patrick, followed by my moving back to care for both my parents. She was baffled by my mother's actions and more so by the fact that my brother Dennis had allowed it to take place.

"I always wished I had a brother or a sister," Kathy commented. "But when I hear stories like this, it makes me grateful to be an only child."

"And I always wished I had a sister," I replied.

We both chuckled over that.

Kathy is still my best friend and the sister I always wanted. I could call her anytime of the day or night if I needed to talk. Just knowing someone was there for me was the greatest blessing.

Lying in bed that night I thought, *It's almost fifty years later, and visiting with Aunt Betty at the hospital that day was still the safest place for me to be.*

Another safe place was only a few weeks away.

I had been seriously contemplating flying back to California to get the remaining items out of storage. It made no sense for me to continue paying $50 a month for the unit. There were enough things in there to warrant the expense and the trip. One of the girls I kept in touch with from the recovery home was a travel agent. I called her and asked about the costs and availability.

She gave me a few dates, but I'd have to leave during the week, and I couldn't afford to miss any days from work. She also had one available seat on a plane leaving for Los Angeles on Saturday morning. It was Memorial Day weekend, and the price was perfect. And the return flight would be Monday. The timing was also perfect. I called the car rental place to reserve a car at the airport.

Lastly, I called the storage place to make sure they'd be open all three days, which they were.

Julie and Steven were two very close friends I had met in recovery; I decided to call them to see if I could spend a few days with them.

"Hi, Julie, guess who this is?"

"Roni, wow, it's so good to hear from you!"

"I'm going to be in Los Angeles this weekend. Can I stay with you and Steven?"

"Of course. You know you always have a place here with us."

"I can't wait to see you."

"Would you like us to pick you up at the airport?" Julie asked.

"I appreciate the offer, but I've already made reservations to rent a car. I'm hoping to get all my belongings out of storage. Since it's Memorial Day weekend, I'll have the extra day to go through it and pack everything up."

I was excited about seeing Julie and Steven and at the same time putting this ordeal behind me.

I arrived in L.A. at 11 a.m. With limited time, I drove directly to the storage facility and immediately started tossing. By noon, the dumpster was half full with my belongings. There was an ironing board, books, radio, clothes, nightstands, an electric tabletop grill all in the trash.

Three hours later, I felt as though I was suffocating in that storage unit. I was drenched with sweat and exhausted from the heat. Before my heart gave out, I had to lock the door and get away from there. How many more times would I be forced to prune away my past and bid farewell to what little I had?

Arriving at Julie's would be the perfect antidote. Walking into the house was like collapsing into a warm, cozy recliner. The tension immediately began to dissipate as they welcomed me with hugs and happy smiles. I showered quickly, and then we left for the evening church service. All the stress was gone as I basked in the safety of the Lord's presence and joined in the praise and worship.

Afterward, Steven grilled steak, shrimp, and veggies for dinner. I took a power nap, and then we all headed out to a midnight candlelight AA meeting. It felt so right to be back with them, and in that meeting, New Jersey was a world away.

Sunday, I awakened early and returned to the storage facility and the sickening job of throwing my possessions away. Steven came over around ten o'clock. I purchased a dozen large boxes, and we packed up the remaining items for Steven to ship back to New Jersey.

> I hope to visit you while passing through and to have you assist me on my journey there, after I have enjoyed your company for a while.
>
> Romans 15:25 (NIV)

After lunch, Steven suggested we take a ride into L.A. An hour later, we entered a beautiful park in Pacific Palisades. It was déjà vu as it reminded me of the Japanese Gardens tucked away in the San Fernando Valley. This was the Gandhi World Peace Memorial, which enshrines a portion of the ashes of Mahatma Gandhi. This place of serenity and magnificence was hidden on the busiest, noisiest, and most well-known street in the world, Sunset Boulevard.

Steven knew how very much I needed this place of peace—this place of *silence*. We took opposite paths. The entire park was empty, as though God knew I needed to be alone. For two hours, I strolled around taking in the beauty of a Windmill Chapel, the floating island bird refuge, the sunken gardens and pathways lined with all the wonders God created. Nothing profound happened. I did not feel any great enlightenment, but I experienced a great sense of calm.

On the way out, I picked up a pamphlet entitled *Gandhi Speaks* containing selections from his writings. This man, who was of another religion, had much to say about *silence*. If ever I was uncertain about who was directing my path, every doubt left me that day.

"After I had practiced silence for some time, I saw the spiritual value of it. It suddenly flashed across my mind that that was the time when I could best hold communion with God," wrote Mahatma Gandhi.

Reading that triggered a memory of Patrick sitting with his head resting in his hands and knowing he too was holding communion with God in his silence.

Julie was home from work when we returned. Steven barbequed chicken, and we relaxed under the stars for the remainder of the evening. I had only one thing left to do—take a midnight swim.

After a few hours of restful sleep, I drove the car to the rental office and boarded the plane back to New Jersey. California would always be home to me. I knew after this weekend, I would return there someday.

The trip had been an emotional and draining ordeal. I had used my entire tax refund and would owe Steven the cost of shipping the boxes. However, getting all my personal mementos and photo albums comforted me.

> Forgetting what is behind and straining toward what is ahead.
>
> Philippians 3:13 (NIV)

It was clear that God had orchestrated things in such a way that I had to go back and do this myself. He had provided me with the strength, the friends, and the resources.

Back in my apartment by late Monday, I had just enough time to catch my breath before I returned to work the following morning.

MY FIRST CAMPING TRIP

I had signed up to go on a camping trip the following weekend with several people from church. I left work an hour early on Friday and drove to Stokes National Forest. Several people went early that morning to set up the tents and unload the food. I chuckled pulling into the parking lot. I thought I had landed on the moon. This huge area had mushroom-like tents of varying sizes, shapes, and colors popping out of the ground for as far as the eye could see. I had a single tent all to myself.

At eight o'clock, we gathered around the campfire and ate hamburgers and hot dogs. By ten o'clock, the kids had worn themselves out, and it became quiet.

Looking up at the stars, I prayed, "Lord, help ease the heaviness of my hurt and show me how to be still so I can hear you."

When Pastor Kevin began to play the guitar softly, I could feel the Spirit flow through me, igniting the desire to join the others as they sang praise and worship songs.

The world vanished as my entire being became still. I didn't sense anyone being near me. I felt God's presence.

The hedge of protection I heard mentioned in prayers was around me that night. I felt safe for the first time in years, maybe the first time ever. Clearly, the Lord had chosen these strangers to shield me and protect me.

By midnight, the yawns had won out. No penthouse on earth could have offered the warmth and love I felt in my little "pent-tent" that night. Suddenly, I knew who it was who had whispered to me, "Pack your thermals." The temperatures had dropped drastically. I felt as though I was the lost sheep. He carried me back to my tent. I fell asleep in the warmth of his arms and in my long johns.

Saturday, we were up bright and early. I couldn't believe the breakfast they served—bacon, eggs, toast, hash browns, coffee, fruit, and juice. No hotel restaurant could serve better, and being outdoors provided a refreshing ambiance. Afterward, we joined for a brief time of prayer.

Each of us was assigned a two-hour slot to prepare a meal for the entire group. There were five in a group. I was given the dinner slot, which would start at 4 p.m.

The pastor led us on a mini-hike up the Appalachian Trail. I never before appreciated the beauty of the hills and valleys with all their contrasting colors. Everything before me was brand new. Still I found myself more fascinated with watching Pastor David. That godly man, whom I had only seen clothed in a suit and tie, was now garbed in army fatigues and matching cap. Two little boys joined the ranks behind their father, leaving their angelic smiles and halos home for the weekend. For two days, they showed the rest of us they were normal, fun-loving, and playful kids.

We joked and laughed while snapping silly pictures. George teetered on the edge of a huge rock pretending he was about to dive off the cliff into the backdrop of mountains and trees extended over the valleys and lakes. Tom stood nearby making weird faces for the camera as the birds flew overhead like part of an immense mobile.

On the drive back, we stopped to watch a baby cub romping around in the woods. A mile down the path, two deer appeared, loping before us with their beauty and grace.

> As the deer pants for streams of water, so my soul pants for you, O God. My tears have been my food day and night.
>
> Psalm 42:1, 3 (NIV)

Is that desire to want, to know, to crave, in the same manner David, the psalmist, describes instinctual? Is it a natural desire? Nothing could describe the depth of my wanting until I read that psalm. *Pant* depicts a powerful picture—knowing what it's like to gasp for a breath of air, thirst in the desert, the parched dry mouth, desperate to lick just a few drops of dew. My insides screamed, but to let go with complete abandon, to set free the words and the emotions and allow them to take flight wouldn't come. "Lord, I need you so much," I whispered. "Only your fountain of living water can quench my desire."

We arrived back at the campsite around one o'clock. The buffet lunch was set on the picnic tables.

Afterward, we drove to the nearby lake. I chose a secluded area. I wanted to be alone and enjoy the solitude and peace the surrounding beauty offered.

How many years had it been since I had lain on a beach and watched people swimming? Only in my dreams had I envisioned myself lying by a lake or an ocean far from the masses of inmates and guards and the groaning sound of steel bars.

As a kid growing up, I loved to watch all the Esther Williams movies. Swimming had been one of my favorite activities, and she was a magnificent swimmer. I'd fantasize that I was Esther Williams as I watched her beau dive into the pool and swim toward her.

It made me think that God's presence was sweeter now than ever. Would I have felt like this if I hadn't been in prison? Definitely not!

I swam several laps in the lake. I floated on the water, mesmerized by the changing sky. The playful game took on new meaning, knowing who was behind the mysteriously changing cloud formations that looked like a palace, that gradually became a cathedral, and then, just as suddenly, changed to splendid waterfalls. I wanted to float there forever.

> I will show wonders in the heavens and on the earth.
>
> Joel 2:30 (NIV)

We arrived back at the site at four o'clock. It was my turn to help prepare dinner. For the next two hours, I worked alongside three women I had never met, but by dinnertime, I felt I had known them all my life.

They were curious about me. I was the mystery woman they had seen every Sunday for the past six months, who sat up front and left immediately after the service.

We talked briefly about my reason for moving back to New Jersey and that I had been taking care of my mother.

"What made you come to our church?" Michelle asked.

In relaying the story, I saw the wonder once again of God's ways.

"Last year, I was here taking care of my brother who was very ill," I said. "Mary Elizabeth, the nurse who took care of him until I arrived, told me about the church she attended and offered to take me with her. This happens to be the church."

One of the three women, Sharon, was quite a bit younger than me. She was divorced with two kids, lived with her sister, Michelle, and her family. Michelle was the second woman, and the third was their sister-in-law, Leslie.

I was taken by surprise with their interaction. The ease and respect for one another was evident. They were more like friends than relatives. I hadn't realized that genuine love and support could be found in families. This camping adventure exposed me to many new ideas.

At nine o'clock that evening, a group of people who

had been rehearsing all week put on a fantastic show. They performed several mini-skits, which were super, and we giggled as loud and as hard as the kids. Then we made messy, but scrumptious, s'mores over the campfire. Again, we relaxed on our blankets and chatted while watching the embers slowly burn down.

On Sunday, the pastor held a service on the hillside. Being a visual person, I tried to picture what it was like for the apostles sitting on the mountainside with people gathered to listen to Jesus preach the beatitudes. Having just read Emmet Fox's *The Sermon on the Mount*, that hour, on that mountaintop, served as a stunning portrayal of the lessons taught two thousand years ago—the reality of living a happy life.

Being out in the fresh air stimulated our appetites. Experiencing that hour on the hillside was uplifting. We walked down from the hillside spiritually satisfied. Our appetites invigorated, we joined together in fellowship while enjoying a hearty breakfast of pancakes, sausage, and eggs.

> This is the day the Lord has made; let us rejoice and be glad in it.
>
> Psalm 118:24 (NIV)

I knew that day that I could pull every petal off every daisy and with absolute certainty say, *He loves me. He loves me. He loves me. And yes, he loves me, a sinner, just as I am.* I found love in the right place on a hillside that day.

We all pitched in after breakfast to clean up. Following that we began to pack up. The tents were all taken down. The canopy over the food area was dismantled.

What had looked like the moon two days prior looked so barren as we pulled away, and there wasn't one thing left in the area where we had stayed.

I wouldn't have wanted to stay any longer. The area we left was now barren, but there was another area inside of me that was filled with emotion. I had spent forty-eight hours experiencing an entirely different way of life. All of it was foreign to me. God was in the center; I had met new people and come away with new friends. I saw families together enjoying each other's company, and the best part: this was just the beginning.

I was glad to get home to shower and unpack. I had the whole evening alone to absorb every detail of the past two days. I had time alone with God. I felt like a new person.

Thinking back on my early days in recovery, I remember having hope for the first time ever. Now I was seeing the aftereffects of that hope. These were not experiences I would have chosen. But that's the glory of allowing God to take charge. What I would have chosen couldn't come close to the glorious weekend I had just encountered.

I had only been on my own for two months, and this was a freedom like nothing I had ever experienced. Certainly walking away from the prison I knew what freedom was like. But I had nothing to look forward to. Now everything was new and exciting. It was pure joy to get up each morning and wait to see what adventure God was planning for me. What would he surprise me with today? I didn't have to wait very long. Every day was a new beginning for me. What many see as routine, I was seeing as a whole new life.

THE COUP DE GRÂCE!

Mom moved into an assisted living home the last week of June. I could not imagine what it was like for her to walk out of a home she had lived in for fifty-one years and an hour later walk into the one place she dreaded more than anything in the world.

The following Saturday, Sharon and I went to the shore. We had breakfast on the boardwalk. Then we went bike-riding for an hour and watched the Fourth of July parade.

On Sunday, I went to church.

"Hey, Roni, are you busy this afternoon?" George asked.

"No, what's going on?"

"About six of us are going to meet at the park for a picnic and watch the fireworks."

"That sounds wonderful. Just give me a call and let me know what time."

We met around five o'clock, with blankets, chairs,

and games, and as I was beginning to see, church people commune around food. I had brought chips and dip; they had brought cheese, fruit, and cookies. For three hours, we did that weird thing—we had fun—we laughed.

Yes, I was the fifty-ish woman going on ten. I saw fireworks that evening that were more spectacular than any I'd seen in the past. I saw wonders around me that I had never noticed before. I heard the crickets chirping. I listened, I watched, and I witnessed the splendor of this new world.

When the fireworks ended, none of us wanted to go home; it was only nine thirty. We decided to go to a show, but the movie we wanted to see didn't start until eleven o'clock, so we headed to the ice cream parlor.

Lying in bed that night, I thought what a wonderful day it had been. The fireworks were the best I had ever seen. Was the day really that awesome, or could it be that now that I had God in my life, everything was so much better?

With it being the holiday weekend, I had Monday off. I got up early and went to visit my mother. She seemed very resigned to her new surroundings. Still, it was obvious she was very lonely.

She was in a room that was farthest from the dining area. She couldn't walk it alone because of her eyesight; an aide had to accompany her. She was paying extra to have breakfast brought to her room.

"I can't do it three times a day. It's so exhausting," she said.

I felt sorry for her, but there was nothing I could do.

My sister-in-law arrived about an hour later. The three of us had a nice chat.

Carol and I left at the same time.

"Carol, I really miss the kids," I said. "Would it be possible for me to see them?"

"Sure," she responded. "We're going on vacation this week. I'll call you when we get back."

"Thank you, God," I said softly to myself. I hadn't seen the kids in more than two months.

A few days later, Mom called me.

"Would you come up Sunday and have lunch with me?" she asked.

"Sure."

A few days after that visit, she called again.

"Roni, please come up some night and have dinner with me," she asked.

I couldn't get there fast enough.

The daytime visits were strained. When I went for dinner it wasn't too bad. I didn't actually eat with her. I sat at her table, and she introduced me to all the other ladies. None of them made any effort to converse. How much is there to talk about?

The following weekend, I went to visit again.

"Eric came to visit and took me out to lunch," she said. "Dennis came too."

The possibility of her enjoying all of us together and sharing a few laughs was history. She had built the wall to keep me out, but for each barrier she erected, she also had shut herself in.

"Mom, could you please tell me what I ever did to you to cause you to kick me out?" I asked.

"Well, that wasn't what I meant to happen. Everything got out of hand, and Dennis—"

Before she could finish, I said, "Mom, I don't want to hear about Dennis. You initiated it. To kick me out and then go so far as to change the locks an hour later was pretty vengeful, and for what reason?"

"Well, changing the locks wasn't my idea," she said.

I thought it sounded like Agatha Christie's *Murder on the Orient Express,* where they all plunge the knife in so that no one person could be blamed for the actual death. She was blaming my brother, and my brother was blaming her.

"Well, I was very angry that you went to a motel and wouldn't tell which one," she continued.

"In other words, it wasn't because of anything I failed to do or because I had neglected you!" I said.

She shrugged.

The bubble had burst along with my fantasy that she might just say she was sorry.

I could not decipher which one of us was sicker as I sat there stifling the urge to say, "Mom, you don't belong here. Let me take you home, and I'll move back." That way I could pretend everything was all right and bury my wounded heart even deeper in my chest. She was still having trouble walking to the dining area and complained no one came to visit her. She was so used to the revolving door at home and the constant stream of people and phone calls.

Three days later, another call!

"No one talks at the lunch table," she complained. "Will you come up Saturday and have lunch with me?"

"Sure."

She sat with the same women at every meal. They seldom made any effort to visit one another in their rooms.

With hindsight, I realize that not only did I allow her to manipulate me, I jumped at every chance to make her happy.

Most of the time she spent listening to audio books on cassettes, and I continued running to four different libraries to get them for her.

At the time it never occurred to me that I had the right to refuse to visit her. It was so inbred in me to make her happy. Or at least try.

It would have been nice to pick her up and go for a ride to the shore and have lunch. Or go visit one of her friends. Unfortunately, I couldn't risk putting myself in a situation where I might be accused of any wrongdoing. I had a horrible fear of offering to take her then having a difficult time getting her to go back.

I had hoped by now that someone in the family would act as a mediator so we could all be together occasionally. Two months passed, and I still had not heard from my sister-in-law about visiting with the kids. I'd have to settle for seeing them at my niece's birthday party in a few weeks.

I had so much compassion for my mother that setting boundaries to protect myself was difficult. It's not a fun way to live when you cease to be able to laugh or joke around or say, "Let's go get some ice cream then sit in the park and feed the ducks."

Recalling the story of Ulysses, I thought, I am Ulysses.

> When Ulysses and his men set out on their journey of conquest, they were warned by Circe to avoid the sirens at all costs. Circe told them that the sirens' voices were alluring but fatal to

all who stopped to listen. The unfortunate listeners became rooted like a tree and could not tear themselves away, until they died of hunger.

"Fill your companions' ears with wax," she counseled. "If you yourself want to listen to their song, first let your men bind you securely to the mast." Ulysses heeded her advice. "If the melody beguiles me," he ordered his men, "I charge you to disobey my word, and bend more strongly to your oars."

At long last, Ulysses heard the beautiful strains that stole into his mind, overpowered his body, and overcame his will. As the music came sweeter and sweeter, Ulysses' love for home weakened. He struggled with his shame, but at last the bewitching voices of the sirens prevailed.

"Loose me and let me stay with the sirens!" he raged. He threatened and entreated; he promised his men mountains of gold with desperate signs and gestures. His men bound him more securely. He raged and tore at his bonds, for it was agony for him. Only after the music died away did they loose him. He had passed out of the zone of temptation.

Would I ever pass out of my mother's hold on me? No! Not yet!

Immediately after church the following Sunday, I found my car on automatic pilot driving me to "that place" again.

By now it was the second or third week in August.

"I don't feel up to going there," she told me shortly after I arrived.

"You don't feel like going where?" I asked.

"Eric and Kim are picking me up at two o'clock to take me to Ashley's birthday party," she said.

It felt like someone had swung a sledgehammer into my chest. My niece's birthday was two weeks away.

"My son and daughter-in-law are picking you up to go to Ashley's birthday party?" I asked.

I really had to struggle to keep my composure, and then I just lost it. I was sobbing. Not in a billion years would I have believed there was the slightest chance that I would not be included. Regardless of what was going on, I was still Ashley's aunt, and to have a party and invite the entire family, and all the relatives and friends, including my son and his wife and intentionally exclude me was sadistic.

"What's the big deal?" she asked. "Dennis is not going either."

I didn't respond; I was so devastated. She couldn't distinguish the difference between the two. Dennis was still licking his wounds and refused to step foot in that house. He couldn't accept that his wife wanted no part of him and had filed for divorce. He had been invited but chose to celebrate with his daughter alone a few days later.

Five days before, she had been begging me to have dinner with her, but today I wasn't good enough to break bread with.

This was my only niece, and I was her only aunt on her father's side.

The only difference between Cinderella and me was that I had no fairy godmother to wave a magic wand to rescue me from this asylum.

"My God, Mom, what did you tell everyone that could make them hate me this much? What did I ever do to you to deserve anything like this?" I asked. "All I did from the day I set foot in New Jersey was to serve you and help you. And *I loved you.*"

She never did answer me.

I wanted to beg for forgiveness, not for any specific wrongdoing, other than the crime of just being born.

My son and his wife were leaving to vacation in France the following day. Ashley's party had been arranged to accommodate them. I had called Eric a few days prior and suggested we get together before they leave. Now I understood the message he had left me. They were going to be busy up until they left. Yeah, spending the day at my only niece's birthday party!

This possibility had never entered the realm of my thinking. Just the year before, when my father was in the hospital, I had been the one driving my mother to Ashley's birthday party. I was also invited to spend Thanksgiving at Carol's parents' home two years in a row. The picture was clear now; I was never the daughter or aunt or sister being invited or welcomed. I was just included because my parents needed a chauffeur.

"I'm leaving," I said.

I could not be there when my son arrived and watch the three of them take off for the party. I left there shattered.

It had been four months since I had seen my son. Physically and emotionally, I was spent. I sent them an e-mail wishing them a safe trip and a wonderful vacation.

Nothing anyone said could ever fill the hole left in my heart after this.

Most people have never experienced the real agony and torture of being removed and isolated from the outside world. I know firsthand the torment and longing to be amongst your loved ones again.

Several years ago, former American prisoners of war were interviewed to determine what methods used by the enemy had been most effective in breaking their spirit. Researchers learned that the prisoners didn't break down from physical deprivation and torture as quickly as they did from solitary confinement or from being frequently moved around and separated from friends. My family did come very close to breaking me. For all the wrongs that they had conjured up and felt I deserved to be hated and punished for, nothing I ever did or could do comes close to what they did to me.

If I live to be a thousand, I will never forget one second of that horrible wanting and the loneliness and the emptiness. I spent sixty seconds of every minute, sixty minutes of every hour, twenty hours of every day, seven days a week hoping and praying and hurting and longing to have my freedom back. I prayed for the day to come when I would be able to hug my kids, kiss them, and tell them how much I love them. I could think of nothing else. I lived and breathed for that moment. And now my mother was doing this to me again.

So much of my life had been determined in an instant. When they put those handcuffs on me, when Dennis took the keys away from me, my life would be filled with unbearable pain and more precious time wasted, all in an instant.

This was the *coup de grâce!*

For a mother to inflict that same punishment on her only daughter a second time without any justification was incomprehensible to me. I have wished a million times over that she had beaten me instead. When you break a person's arm, you break their arm, but when you slander a person, you ruin their life.

My mother had a real talent for playing on people's sympathy, and it became addictive and seductive to her.

A few days later, she was calling again.

"I'm still having pain," she said. "I'm not too sure about the doctor taking care of me here."

I grew concerned thinking that possibly the cancer had spread to the abdomen and we were overlooking the obvious.

"Mom, I'm at work now, but I can pick you up and bring you back here to see Dr. Lane," I said.

"No, I'll wait a few hours and see how I feel," was her final response.

Meanwhile, I called the oncologist's office. I knew the girl who worked there, and she agreed to fax over all my mother's records. I pulled all the pertinent information from the chart we had in the office and faxed everything to the doctor at the nursing home. He called and thanked me.

Two hours later, I got an emergency call from the head nurse at the nursing home telling me my cousin was there to take my mother to the hospital. I was disappointed that my mother chose to call my cousin so soon after I offered to go pick her up.

Unable to reach Dennis on his cell phone, I called Todd in Washington. I started to cry as I told him of my suspicions.

"Maureen called me early this morning and told me she was taking Mom to the hospital," he said.

I do not recall one word either of us said after that, I was so stunned. With the time difference between Washington and New Jersey, it was clear these plans had already been made when I spoke to my mother. Maureen would call Todd three thousand miles away, but she wouldn't call me fifteen miles away. Instead, I got an emergency call at work.

Once again, I had been pulled in by events too complex to understand yet too powerful to protest.

I still could not keep myself from going to see her. I went up that night, and she seemed to be okay.

Based on all the records I faxed to the doctor, he ordered a CAT scan.

The following evening, we were told the results showed the cancer had spread to the abdomen. Although I had thought it was a possibility, I wasn't prepared for the reality.

I went to work the following morning but left at noon.

I was a nervous wreck driving to the hospital. I just didn't know how to face my mother after all that had gone on these past few months.

As I was approaching the entrance of the hospital, I saw a familiar figure sitting on the bench, and it took a second to register that it was Alan. He was the fellow who played the drums in the church band. He and his girlfriend, Cecile, attended the Life Group with me every Thursday night.

"You never know who you'll run into around here," I said to him.

He was just as surprised to see me.

"Are you here visiting someone too?" I asked.

"No, I work here," he said. "How about you?"

"My mom is in here," I said.

Undoubtedly, God had put Alan right in my path.

Alan sensed my tension.

"Would you like me to go up with you?" he asked.

"You know, Alan, I really would appreciate that," I said.

Alan's presence cushioned what could have been a very awkward situation. Mom could see his shadow. I introduced them.

"Alan plays the drums at church on Sunday," I said.

She went on to tell him all about my brother Dennis playing the drums when he was in high school and how the noise almost lifted the roof off the house. They talked about the audio books the Library of Congress lends to the blind at no cost. Alan had worked for the Post Office and told her they used to come in by the pallet.

"They took me down for X-rays this morning, but there was a problem," she said.

"I work in the X-ray department," Alan said. "We had equipment problems due to the heavy rains last night."

After he left, Mom talked nonstop for the next hour giving me every detail of the audio book I had bought her the week before.

"I'm starting to get some pain," she said.

I buzzed the nurse, and she came in and gave her a shot.

"Mom, I'm so sorry about the results," I said.

She seemed very resigned to it and just hoped it wasn't going to be a long drawn-out ordeal. She talked about returning to the assisted living home.

It had been a nice visit, and I was grateful for Alan's intervention.

Saturday, my Aunt Betty and her daughter, Kathy, picked me up to go to the hospital. I had mentioned on the drive up that Mom still had a little bit of an appetite and that she enjoyed the milkshakes we brought up to her. When we arrived at the hospital, I went up with my aunt, and Kathy went to get my mother a milkshake.

"Hi, Mom. Aunt Betty is here," I said. "Kathy went to get you a milkshake."

"Is she in the kitchen making it?" she asked.

She was a little out of it. She perked up a bit when Kathy came in with the milkshake.

We stayed for an hour. It was a nice visit.

Sunday, I went to church and then to the hospital. Todd had arrived. Mom seemed more alert.

Carol arrived with the kids; I was happy to see them. They stayed for about an hour.

"I'll be back tomorrow, Helen," Carol said.

However my mother responded, Carol misunderstood her and thought my mother was trying to rush her out.

"Gee, Helen, are you kicking me out?" she asked teasingly.

My mother lifted her head off the pillow and gently cupped Carol's face in her hands and kissed her.

"I would never kick you out, Carol!" she said.

My heart stopped! That scene would be forever etched in my memory. I wanted so much to say, "You don't have to worry, Carol. She only kicks her own daughter out!"

Never in my entire life had my mother taken my face in her hands and looked at me so tenderly and told me she loved me.

The following morning, I got a call at work.

"Todd just called from the hospital. Mom is screaming in excruciating pain with both her legs," Dennis said.

I left work immediately. She was still screaming when I got there, but not quite as bad. We assumed it was her circulation. They had given her a shot, but she was still in pain.

I started to massage her leg.

"Don't touch me," she said.

Dennis arranged for a masseuse to come. The fellow arrived about an hour later and massaged her legs for quite a while. She would let a stranger touch her but not me.

Todd left the following morning to return to Washington.

The X-rays showed she had a blood clot in her leg.

Eric and Kim were due to return from France that day. I left a few messages to call me at the hospital.

"Hi, Mom, we're home," Eric said.

"I'm with Grandma now. She's sleeping," I said. I filled him in with all the details.

"We'll get the five o'clock bus out of Port Authority and be in Union by six o'clock," he said.

"Okay, I'll pick you up."

We arrived back at the hospital around seven o'clock.

A short time later, Carol arrived, followed by Dennis and then my cousin Maureen.

"Let's all go into the conference room," Maureen said. I was shunted to the sidelines, the helpless observer in this battle I wasn't trained to fight.

"I've been in touch with your mom's doctor, and he feels we should wait another day before starting the IV morphine drip," Maureen continued.

"Absolutely not," Dennis and I said in unison. We had

been watching her for two days, and it made no sense to allow her to go through another night of pain.

"I'll call the doctor," Maureen said. "Roni, I hope there are no hard feelings about me taking care of all this?"

"Not at all," I said. I was tempted to say, "Stop testing me."

"I'm going to remain here," Dennis announced. "I'm here for the duration."

Did that mean till morning or till she passed? No one knew. Unquestionably, it was very admirable. But I knew in my heart of hearts, I was being set up for the kill. He would stay until morning and expect me to take over. I never said one word or gave the slightest indication that I would be back in the morning, simply because I did not intend to go back there in the morning.

This was no longer an option for me. I worked for four doctors in an extremely busy office. The girls in the office had been wonderful covering for me. I had to go in for a few hours.

I didn't know whether my mother would last a minute, the night, or a week. She could very well last another six months or longer. I had rent to cover and bills to be paid, and I had already taken off more time than I should have.

I went into work early. I called Dennis at nine o'clock.

"How's Mom doing?" I asked.

"She slept through the night," he said.

When he heard I was at work, I could feel the heat through the receiver, and he slammed the phone down.

I sat at my desk fighting back the tears. I pleaded with God to give me the strength to get through this. I will never forget asking, "What would you do, Jesus?"

About fifteen minutes later, Janet, the receptionist, was on her way up to get coffee.

"How are you doing?" she asked.

I told her what happened.

"Janet, I don't know what the right thing to do is anymore," I said. "If I don't go there, I know it's only out of spite because I'm so angry with my brother, but I really want to be there. I also know I can't be walking out of here again with all the work I have backed up on my desk."

"Roni, you go there and don't worry about your brother or the work," she said.

God had answered me. Through Janet, I knew exactly what Jesus would do.

When I arrived, Dennis was reading his newspaper and had settled down. My mother was still sleeping.

I called a priest and asked if he would come give my mother the last rites, which he did.

"Your mom was crying out during the night for her mother," the girl in the other bed told me.

How interesting that, at the age of eighty-five, she would call for her mother. Would I do the same thing someday, or was I finally willing to accept the futility of my bid for her love? I had been calling out to her my whole life.

I went back to my reading but kept looking up at her. Around three o'clock, when I glanced up at her, she looked like a ghost; there was absolutely no color in her. I knew intuitively it was close. I went over and kissed her on the forehead.

"Mom, it's okay for you to go home to be with Dad and Patrick," I said.

Then it was over. I wept as I asked the girl in the next bed to please buzz the nurse.

I called Dennis immediately. I called Eric but was unable to reach him. I called Kim and told her.

"I'm so sorry," she said. "I'll get a hold of Eric."

It was hard to imagine that, exactly one week ago almost to the minute, Alan and I were there and Mom was eating and talking up a storm.

I reached into the drawer of the cabinet next to the bed to get her belongings. Amongst them was a postcard from my son and daughter-in-law from France. They never sent me one. I prayed for this to be the last time I would feel this much anguish.

I had loved my mother dearly, but I couldn't wish her back. Her pain and her misery were over. I had no doubt she was with my father and my brother, and she could look down now and see all of us.

I felt a great sense of peace knowing I had been with her and that I had behaved in a respectable manner throughout. I could get on with my life, and the cause for my never- ending hurt and pain was over.

I was wrong. It had just begun, but this time in a very different way.

When I arrived home, I immediately called Kathy, Aunt Betty, and Sharon. Within two hours, they were at my place. Kathy and Aunt Betty came with a casserole of lasagna and Sharon with a cheesecake.

Aunt Betty told Sharon the story of her friendship with my mother and how it all began with, "Yoo-hoo, my name is Helen."

We had a good laugh over that, and fortunately, we found enough happy memories to reminisce about.

THE SAME PATH ONE YEAR LATER

I could only pray that my "Conflict of Desires" would end sooner rather than later. I wanted to be in harmony with God. I was ready to move into my spiritual home, *his will*. But there were still so many obstacles in my way.

Dennis and I arranged to meet with the funeral director the following morning. My cousin Maureen offered to drive us. No surprise that she had all my mother's clothes with her when she picked us up. We'd had three wakes in sixteen months at this same funeral home.

Several people from my meetings came. They were a great comfort. Sharon stayed with me for the afternoon. Family members were pleasant as introductions were made.

Todd and Eric gave the eulogies at church. It was exactly one year to the date that I had stood in that same pulpit giving the eulogy for my father.

Following the luncheon, the immediate family all met back at the house.

"Todd, when are you leaving to go home?" I asked.

"Monday morning."

"Could you, Dennis, and I get together?" I asked.

"Is this something I'm going to need my lawyer for?" he responded.

"No, you don't need your attorney. I would like for the three of us to open all the Mass cards and go over a few things."

His reference to my son when he said "lawyer" haunted me for months. *How dare he think he could use my own son to defend him against me?* Yet Eric sat there and never said one word. At the very *least* I expected Eric to say, "Hey, Todd, don't expect me to get involved in this." What he should have said was, "Hey, Todd, it should be obvious that would be a conflict of interest. I'll be advising my mother if she needs any help." Clearly neither happened.

I probably should have been the one to get an attorney.

After agreeing to meet the following evening, I left.

At that moment, I wanted to be as far away from that house as possible, anywhere but in the company of these people, anyplace but New Jersey. It was my mother who was buried in the ground that day. But it was me who was being buried alive mentally and emotionally, carrying the wounds their rejection had embedded in my soul.

Dennis had told me months before my mother passed that she wanted me out of the will.

What a hateful and begrudging legacy she left for me to live with.

Being honest, I had asked to meet Sunday evening for the sole purpose of finding out if I was in the will or not. I didn't want to have to be thinking about it for the next few weeks or until they decided it should be read. I didn't know whether or not my mother had removed me. And if she had I wanted to know and move on.

We concluded our meeting Sunday evening. It really wasn't much of a meeting. We went through the Mass cards. Dennis read the will. And yes, I was still in it. No doubt if my mother had lived longer I would have been removed.

Before my mother went into the nursing home, she had dispersed many of her more valuable items and some furniture that my ex–sister-in-law asked for. My son and his wife got the dining room set, an elegant mahogany bookcase, and several pieces of crystal stemware and Lennox. I got three items that I had to beg for. A little porcelain multicolored flower arrangement, a little jam dish with a spoon from Ireland, and a truffle dish. The three combined didn't come to $50.

"Have a safe flight home, Todd," I said as I kissed him good-bye.

He was the lucky one to be flying home knowing he was his mother's pride and joy and one of her favored children. He didn't have to lift a finger to do anything, and he would still be entitled to a third of the inheritance. Dennis would get his third and take the entire contents of the house, along with a nice amount as the executor. I would remain in a straightjacket called "the past" and desperately wanting to scroll back and edit out the prior fourteen months. I had already paid far more than whatever my third of the inheritance would be.

> Every kingdom divided against itself will be ruined, and every city or household divided against itself will not stand.
>
> Matthew 12:25 (NIV)

The woman who claimed her entire life that all she wanted was to see us happy and for all of us to get along had now succeeded in tearing us asunder.

I once heard a story about a mother who had five children. Following her death, the children were discussing the hours prior to her death, and, in jest, one of them said that Mom told her she was the favorite child.

"That can't be," exclaimed the second child. "She told me I was her favorite."

"You're both wrong; Mom told me I was her favorite," said the third child.

This discourse continued through to the fifth child. On her death bed, the mother called each child in one by one and told him or her that he or she was her favorite. I thought that was the most beautiful story I had ever heard. She wanted each of them to know how much she loved them. They were each, in their own way, her favorite.

My family could take the house and everything in it for all I cared. I thank God I had my new church family and another upcoming surprise.

TENT REVIVAL AND RETREAT

The church I had recently become a member of held an outdoor tent revival at the end of September. I worked as an usher every evening. Reverend Spencer, who was going to be the speaker, was the senior pastor at a church in Massachusetts. Many of his church members were people recovering from addictions and, like all of us, carried a lot of excess baggage. Pastor Spencer's knowledge of the Bible and presentation were incisive. His experience paralleled the listener's, adding validity to what he said. He uncovered secrets buried in places we never knew existed.

> And the secrets of his heart will be laid bare. So he will fall down and worship God, exclaiming, "God is really among you!"
>
> 1 Corinthians 14:25 (NIV)

You could see the truth of that verse just by listening to what Pastor Spencer preached. Messages about recovery are very powerful to me. I've lived it. I know the power of God, and every day, I see and feel the Holy Spirit softening my ways.

Each night, Pastor Spencer ended his message on a high note to ensure our return. It was a ten-night Christian soap opera, and I couldn't wait to get there the following evening and the evening after that.

My new mantra had become, *Thank you, Lord. Thank you, Lord.* I just could not stop thanking him for all the good things, the new people, and the childlike excitement I felt with each new experience. No matter how tired I was after working all day, the minute I pulled into the parking lot and saw the tent, I became energized. My burdens disappeared. I was with my new family and felt comfortable and welcomed and definitely ready to "Shout to the Lord."

The church was on the corner of a main intersection in town, and it did not take long for the people to hear Pastor Spencer's voice booming through the microphones. Each night brought more people, and the following night, they brought their friends. People came from miles around when the word spread and they heard the music. That band rocked! Mick Jagger and his Rolling Stones had nothing on the youth ministry that belted out words of praise and worship to the God whose Spirit swept through that tent.

For most new Christians, I believe we all feel the same when we hear the various messages. It always seems like the preachers know something about us, and their sermons are geared specifically to us.

Even the scriptures Rev. Spencer quoted spoke to me. In hindsight, I know now that each moment had been preplanned with precision. I was far removed from my old ways, and the need to discuss the turmoil I was going through decreased. The conversations in my head continued, but not verbalizing every thought led to a more peaceful time. My mind became clearer through the process of being silent, and I was able to hear and heed the words that were being spoken to me through Pastor Spencer.

> But the Lord is in his holy temple; let all the earth
> be silent before him.
>
> Habakkuk 2:20 (NIV)

That's how I felt every evening as I walked toward that tent. I felt as though I had entered a holy temple. There was an aura of reverence but at the same time an excitement and anticipation of what Pastor Spencer would preach.

The Sunday after he left, I was talking with a friend in the café area of the church. I noticed a flyer with Pastor Spencer's picture lying on the table. The flyer offered what I refer to as a once-in-a-lifetime opportunity: a tour of the Holy Land. He, along with two other pastors from Massachusetts, had arranged a two-week pilgrimage to Israel. I called the travel agency the following day and requested they mail me all the information and a complete itinerary.

Three years earlier, when I had attempted to end my life, the doctor approved visitations by friends, and Debra had raced to the hospital with the shampoo I requested. When she left that afternoon, I immediately opened the bag she had given me. In it were six little bottles of shampoo and conditioners all from hotels in Israel where she and her husband had just been. I thought to myself, *Who would ever want to go on vacation to Israel?*

Now, three years later, I was making plans to go on my first vacation in thirty years. I was going to Israel in the spring.

And in three weeks I would be attending my first retreat sponsored by Alcoholics Anonymous.

My coworkers had taken up a collection after my mother's passing and insisted that I use it for myself. I called Connie immediately.

Connie was a girl I had met in AA. We were the same age and in recent months had become better friends. She had lost her mother the year before. We went to the movies once in a while or out for coffee. She and another mutual friend, Joan, were planning to attend an AA retreat in Staten Island sometime during October. They had asked me to join them, but I didn't have the money. It also meant I'd have to take Friday off. The retreat was from Friday at noon until Sunday at 2 p.m.

"Guess what! I'll be able to go with you and Joan on the retreat," I said. "Connie, do you have any idea how excited I am? The amount my coworkers gave me is the exact cost of the retreat."

"Oh, Roni, I'm thrilled," she said. "You're going to love it."

I had requested Friday off, as we were leaving early for the retreat. I woke before the alarm had a chance to sound its bell. By nine o'clock, my car was packed, and I was dressed and raring to meet with Connie and Joan. At noon, we stopped for pizza, enjoying a leisurely lunch. It was awesome to be with friends whose excitement and enthusiasm matched my own.

> Let us therefore make every effort to do what leads to peace and to mutual edification.
>
> Romans 14:13 (NIV)

We arrived at the retreat house around 3 p.m. We unloaded our bags and immediately went to the conference room. Again, my mouth was gaping, viewing the table filled with all sorts of snacks, candy, and coffee. Within the hour, I had met most of the other fifty women, and in no time, we were old friends. I went into the library and glanced through some books and enjoyed the solitude of this beautiful place away from the hustle and bustle of everyday life.

At six o'clock, I walked across the hills to the cafeteria. Nature had me wrapped in her arms, giving me the opportunity to see, to touch and take in the fragrance of God's presence. I found peace and beauty there. I thanked God with a silent prayer.

It had been suggested that we sit with different people at each meal. We were people in recovery who came together to share our experience, strength, and hope with a mutual feeling of ease and comfortability.

Father Giles was the retreat master—a perfect cutout of what one pictures a little Friar Tuck to look like, with sandals, brown robe, and braided belt, complete with the bald spot.

He captured our attention with his gentle manner and that unique ability to inject humor into his personal experiences. His obvious love for the God he served kept us enthralled during every lecture. The theme for the weekend—humility!

Those who chose to met the following morning in the chapel as we read aloud selected devotions. At eight thirty, we walked to the cafeteria for breakfast. This was followed by another lecture, and then we broke into small groups and went into separate rooms for meetings. These were AA meetings but with people we met there. It was always fun to attend meetings with new people and to listen to them share. Sometimes we were given a specific topic, such as gratitude or sharing what brought us into AA. There were women there from several different areas of New York and New Jersey.

After lunch, we had some free time. Dinner was served at six o'clock, followed by another lecture.

This group had been doing a raffle for many years. We knew in advance to bring one or as many items as we wanted to donate. Nothing too old or used up, books, plaques, jewelry, stuffed animals, the usual foray, and the proceeds were used for future scholarships for girls who could not afford the cost to attend.

Not only was it a worthwhile cause, I can't remember having such a fun time. The girl who had hosted this event for many years had been appropriately named Vanna White. She got up before the group and ad-libbed the funniest descriptions of each item, making it so enticing that you came close to retrieving your own donation. We laughed for two hours. The same four-foot teddy bear that Joan donated and drove there with us would now be driving home with us. I had the winning ticket, and he now belonged to me.

Lying in bed that night, I had mentioned to Connie that the preacher who spoke at the tent revival left flyers about a trip he and a few other pastors were putting together. It was a trip to the Holy Land sometime in March.

"If my mother's house sells and things are settled, I hope to go."

"I'd love to go too," Connie said.

"Wow, wouldn't that be awesome?" I blurted out excitedly. "Just imagine the two of us traveling to Israel."

Sunday morning, we attended mass in the chapel. Then we met for breakfast and one final lecture. Lunch was served at one o'clock. Two hours later, after many good-bye hugs, we were on our way home, much richer spiritually, more blessed than I thought possible, more loved than the day prior and with the joyful anticipation of Connie and me traveling together to Israel in five months.

I couldn't wait to get "home" and think about all the good things I had experienced over the weekend.

Every Thursday evening, I attended the Life Group, and this continued to lift me emotionally and spiritually. I hungered to learn more. The group had been so successful, the pastor decided it was time to split up and form new groups; he referred to this process as cell groups. It was another new experience and a marvelous concept. By dividing our group and offering us a leadership training program, each of us would then form a new group and become the leader.

Every Saturday morning, we met in the church café and watched a John Maxwell leadership video. This man just blew my mind. If I had as much godly knowledge as I had street knowledge, I'd be sitting on the right side! As embarrassing as my life had been, that's how exciting it was for me at this time. We took notes and Pastor Kevin taught additional classes. We were inspired and motivated, yet there was a sadness knowing our group had come to an end.

> There is a time for everything, and a season for every activity under the heaven.
>
> Ecclesiastes 3:1 (NIV)

The humorous side came about watching us recruit people to join our individual groups. Suddenly, our Christian-ness disappeared. Maybe I should speak for myself, when I began passing the word around that I would be serving dinner (just kidding).

Pastor David recommended we have one leader and a co-leader. Michelle and I agreed to be a team, and what a team we became. We jumped in with gusto to win souls and to teach his Word. This period of time truly held the key to a venture that reminded us of what it had been like for the apostles. Certainly, we were the blessed ones. We did not have to go forth in sandals and hide in fear of anyone finding out what we were teaching. The precious gift of freedom!

Every Thursday, we met at my apartment with twelve to sixteen attendees. The blessings and gifts of their shared experiences and knowledge shattered the one thing in my life that needed shattering. God was not a punishing God! He had saturated me with everything and every possible person to make me aware of his love for me. It only took fifty-seven years for this stubborn woman to be reached.

God's infinite patience and love brought me to my knees and my face to the ground many times during these months.

SPASMS OF REJECTION

The cold weather had settled in. Thanksgiving was only three weeks away. I couldn't wait to celebrate the holiday with my son Eric and his wife.

"Hi, Mom, I wanted to let you know Kim and I will be busy Thanksgiving," Eric said. "Garrett is visiting from Los Angeles, and we're all going out for dinner."

Garrett was a close friend of Eric's for years. I knew him very well. He had been in our home many times. They were in high school together and college roommates.

"Could you hold on a minute, Eric?" I asked. "I'll be right back."

"No problem," he said.

Hyperventilating, I was tempted to grab a paper bag because I wasn't sure. Do I breathe in or do I breathe out?

I managed to catch my breath long enough to get through the next few minutes, at the same time shoving the words that were forming on my lips back down my throat and telling myself to lie, lie, lie.

"How long has it been since you've seen him?" I asked.

Whatever his answer, if my life depended on it, I could not remember. I would not let him know how his callousness had affected me. I managed to segue our conversation in another direction.

Eric and I had a conversation months prior when he told me not to worry. He reassured me that Kim would get over whatever it was she was feeling toward me. He also told me she was already making plans for Thanksgiving dinner, and I would be included.

I wish I could find the words, but there weren't any. Even *numb* doesn't come close. Pulverized, maybe? Fortunately, I was alone and at home, because without warning, the internal volcano erupted. The words spewed out with no possibility of controlling them. "Mom," I screamed out loud, "you died with a hatred for me that matches my own hatred of you right now."

Thanksgiving, the myth of tradition, family joined together around the table, with the turkey in the middle, blah, blah, blah. Eric was my son (funny how I feel the need to keep reminding myself of that fact), and he and his wife lived only twenty minutes away. I still could not believe he would leave his own mother alone on my first Thanksgiving following the death of my brother and both of my parents. During her fifty-eight years of marriage, my mother never spent a Thanksgiving or any holiday without her husband and relatives and always, always, always with her children. How many holidays and birthdays had I been the one cooking and serving her royal highness?

But God more than tripled my blessings and covered me on all sides. Three people from church called me the week prior to Thanksgiving and invited me to spend the day with them. Unfortunately, I was not in a place that would allow me to enjoy spending that particular holiday with new friends. They were not strangers, but they did not know what had happened or about the turmoil that was bubbling inside of me. I did not trust my emotional state, so I declined their invitation.

A few days later, Kathy invited me to share Thanksgiving with her and Ken and their two kids, Mary Beth and Kevin. Aunt Betty was there, along with a few of Kathy's friends. We had a wonderful time. That evening, I went to a movie with two friends from church.

The last week of November, my mother's house sold. It had only been on the market for a week. "Thank you, Lord," I said.

As happy as I was, though, it still was another reminder of how isolated I was from my family. I couldn't get past the constant reminders.

Dennis found an apartment and took the two sofas, chairs, two televisions, VCR, stereo, wall unit, bedroom set, dressers, another bed, two end tables, night tables, washer and dryer, refrigerator, all the tools, the Christmas tree and all the decorations, two filing cabinets, shelving, and everything else in the house. He would not allow me in the house.

Why did I always end up fighting for what others just took for granted? After all the months of his abuse, I still could not hurt him. I only knew how to hurt myself.

It was just mind-boggling to think I was her only daughter and the only one who had nothing, yet she would not leave me one thing from that house. No one asked me if there was anything I needed.

I think it was Mark Twain who said, "Each person is born to one possession which out values all the others—his last breath."

If something didn't change soon, I would be taking that last breath.

I heard Betty and James Robeson, the hosts of a popular Christian show, *Life Today,* talk about the son they adopted. And I will never forget listening to Betty tell the audience what the judge told them the day the adoption was finalized, "They could never disown this child or leave him out of their inheritance." Wow!

I did not drink or smoke anymore, I was going to church every Sunday, I had a very respectable and responsible job, and I was not involved with anyone. I lived a decent and clean life, and still my family was punishing me. Because I had done something bad fifteen years prior, I had to pay.

It didn't matter that I had already paid the price by going to prison; now I had to pay for the shame I had brought on my family.

One scripture became my passport to Israel. I knew that Connie and I would be going to the Jordan. And I knew I would reach the land of milk and honey.

> You have not yet reached the resting place and the inheritance the Lord your God is giving you. But you will cross the Jordan and settle in the land the Lord your God is giving you as an inheritance, and he will give you rest from all your enemies around you so that you will live in safety.
>
> Deuteronomy 10: 9, 10 (NIV)

I will never forget one particular scene in a very popular movie, *Guess Who's Coming to Dinner*. The movie is about a white girl who brings her African-American boyfriend, played by Sidney Poitier, home to meet her unsuspecting parents.

Later in the movie, there's a very profound scene that takes place between Sidney Poitier and his father. His father is about to lay the guilt on him, and Sidney Poitier stops him in mid-sentence and says:

> You listen to me. You say you don't want to tell me how to live my life, so what do you think you've been doing? You tell me what rights I've got or haven't got and what I owe you for what you've done for me. Let me tell you something. I owe you nothing if you carried that bag a million miles. You did what you were supposed to do, because you brought me into this world and from that day you owed me everything you could ever do for me. Like I will owe my son, if I ever have one. But you don't own me. You can't tell me when or where I'm out of line or try to get me to live my life according to your rules. You don't even know what I am, Dad. You don't know who I am. You don't know how I feel or what I think. And if I tried to explain it the rest of my life, you will never understand. You are thirty years older than I am. You and your whole lousy generation believe the way it was for you is the way it's got to be. And not until your whole generation has lain down and died will the dead weight of you be off our backs. Do you understand? You've got to get off my back!

That scene lasted a minute and a half, and those were my sentiments exactly.

I was not shown one ounce of respect or allowed any privacy. My life and every move I made were told to anyone and everyone my mother spoke to. While I was still living with Mom, she told me that my cousin Maureen had asked her how much I was making.

"You didn't tell her, did you?" I said.

"Of course I did," she responded.

My mother's idea of respecting my privacy was for her only to repeat to ten people instead of twenty what none of them had a right to know or more importantly, ask.

A few months prior, Dennis told me the family all thought I had moved back so I could live the easy life while Mom paid for everything. Then, when I got the job, I was informed that the family was furious that I was leaving Mom alone. It was a no-win situation.

The description of most parents by Tony Campolo, a Christian professor, is right on the mark, "Parents have kids so they have someone to love them and for emotional gratification and emotional fulfillment. Meanwhile, that puts a tremendous amount of pressure on the child. The child's whole meaning in life becomes tied up in making his parents happy."

Bingo! I had been tied up for fifty years trying to please my mother and to what end? I saw the same pattern in Dennis but never with Patrick or Todd. They just had to walk in the door or call once a week. There was never any physical exertion on their part to try to make their parents happy. My parents accepted them and loved them.

Campolo noted that parents want their kids to be rich, prestigious, and successful. They expect from their kids what the dominant society dictates. I recalled the times my mother revealed the truth of her jealousy over how successful my kids had become. On the flip-side, all I could remember was the importance that was placed on religion when we were children. I was left thunderstruck with this recent conflict. On the side of religion, I had been doing all the right things, but little by little, I began to see that religion was of paramount importance to my father, never my mother.

In her twisted mind, I was neither successful nor prestigious, and since religion wasn't important to her, I was a nothing. And the fact that this lowlife daughter could rear two successful sons was more than she could digest.

As Campolo states further, when children fall radically in love with Jesus, they don't give a hoot what society thinks, and immediately they are at odds with their parents.

I had somehow been straddling the middle ground. I definitely loved Jesus, but I was far from radical in that love.

Charles Cooley, Campolo says, developed what is called the "Cooley Looking Glass Self-Concept." Let us say a person's self-concept is determined by what the most important person in his life thinks of him. So, for most of us as young children, it's our mother or father. Later on, it's friends. Already, we can see what the problem is for many of us. My concept of self was hideous; it always had been.

I reared my children as best I could. I would not have abandoned them for anything in this world. And when the time came for them to make their own choices, I let them make them. They are who they are today because

I gave them that freedom. However, as their mother, I do deserve their respect. And that's the part that hurt so bitterly, when I realized being with me for one holiday was asking too much.

The Fifth Commandment says, "Honor thy Father and thy Mother." Does "honor" mean giving up your life and moving back with your parents to help them by becoming their slaves? Nowhere in the Bible does it say we should become subservient to our parents. We are to respect them.

I don't recall reading in the Bible where Mary looked at her son hanging on the cross and said, "Oh, Jesus, why didn't you just stay home and be a carpenter like your father?" Nor did she say, "Oh, Jesus, how could you do this to me?" Leaving his family at thirty and going off to preach was not about her. Jesus was brought into this world for a reason and a purpose. His destiny was to die on the cross for our salvation, and as much pain as that caused Mary, she had to accept it as part of a far greater plan than any of us could imagine. And there is no difference between Jesus's life and our own children's lives. God did not give me the honor of birthing Chad and Eric so they could become who I thought they should become, only what their heavenly Father intended.

I don't lay claim to be any paragon of virtue, and I don't need any reminders of my past behavior, but I could never have banished my kids as my mother did me. My methods were wrong, but the message was clear. I would do whatever was necessary to keep them with me and provide for them.

I had been banished from my mother's home and her life. And just six short months later, I would be forced to accept it was the beginning of the end between my son and me.

I once heard a preacher say we can be given seventeen positive affirmations and all it takes is one negative comment to cancel out all of those affirmations. I remember thinking at the time that I would have been thrilled with just one positive affirmation. My mother's ratio was one hundred negative to zero positive.

I cannot recall one activity I ever engaged in that she sat on the sidelines and encouraged me or applauded me. Yet, when the greatest joy of my life arrived, and I gave birth to Chad, the first grandchild, Mom was right there to tell me how homely he was.

My mother could say or do anything she wanted without any thought of how much she had hurt me. My son would exclude me from his life as if I never existed.

Eric had no idea what he had unleashed. I had to initiate the greatest of restraint to keep from exploding and letting Eric know exactly what I thought of him. In thinking back on these times, it becomes very clear yet again that only through the grace of God was I able to hold my tongue. The need for silence was becoming more evident, and the ability to remain silent was a gift from God. I could never have done this without him.

I would soon learn that God has a sense of humor, and what he sets in motion leaves nothing to chance. We will be where he intends for us to be.

ESTHER AND NORTH CAROLINA

The Saturday after Thanksgiving I went to the church café early, thinking we were having a follow-up training session for our Life Group. I was so looking forward to the fellowship. The pastor always brought coffee and donuts. One thing I was definitely learning was fellowship meant eating. And we were fellowshipping an awful lot in recent months. I kept waiting for everyone else to arrive. Five minutes went by, then ten, and still no one appeared.

Finally the door opened and in walked the pastor's wife. "Hi, Noel. What am I missing here?" I asked.

"There is no training this morning," she replied. "We're having our annual Foursquare Metro meeting here this morning with all the women from the Gathering Place. We meet here the last Saturday of October every year."

The Gathering Place was the church we visited while on the bus trip with the women. As she was telling me this, several kids from the youth ministry were coming in with trays of sandwiches and salads, along with soda pop and paper plates.

"If you'd like, Noel, I'll be glad to help set up, and then I'll split."

Before we knew it, people were arriving, and I was still setting up, looking even worse than when I arrived. The women were all dressed very nicely, and the men were in suits and ties.

"Noel, I'm going to slip out now," I said.

By this time, I had already been introduced to most of the women, and they insisted I stay. The men went upstairs to a meeting room with Pastor David.

The purpose of the women's meeting was to prepare for the upcoming retreat. I sat way back in the corner captivated by the elaborate plans for a show they were putting on in the theme of Esther. *Who was Esther?*

Pastor Carol from the Gathering Place church began showing swatches of purple velvet that she planned to use for the backdrop setting. She showed the most awesome blueprints of rooms from Solomon's Temple. I retreated even farther back in my little corner, not having a clue who Solomon was or what this temple was all about.

The drawings were a recreation of individual rooms displaying the gold jars and treasure chests overflowing with jewelry and strings of pearls. I'm not kidding when I say this appeared to be as magnificent as any plans for a Broadway production.

Once the details were complete, they went on to discuss some other ideas and plans. Pastor Carol asked if anyone would be willing to bake cookies. They needed several women to volunteer to bake about two hundred cookies each. She explained that following the first show on Friday evening, the women would return to their rooms and change into their pajamas. They would then be assigned to meet with a few other women to "kick back" and discuss their thoughts on the presentation. This was called "Snuggle Time," and each woman would be given a little bag with homemade cookies along with a small container of milk.

It was as though my hand had a mind of its own, and before I was even aware of it, my arm was in the air. "I'll be happy to help. In fact, I'll bake all the cookies," I offered.

Well, I baked and I baked every evening and weekend for the next three weeks. I baked cookies until my oven broke. I bought little cellophane Christmas bags, tied ribbons around five hundred bags, and curled every bow. I packed those bags as protectively and carefully as though they were my firstborn. And I personally carried ten cartons to the bus the day of departure to make sure the bus driver put them in a compartment where nothing could disturb "my cookies."

I would bake a million cookies for the reward the Lord blessed me with that weekend. Noel insisted I go as their guest. I attended that same retreat for the next three years.

The women from the Gathering Place don't call me by name; in fact, they don't even know my name. I am *The Cookie Lady*—a title I cherish, a title I'm proud of, because I did my little bit for his kingdom. As Mother Teresa said, "We don't have to do big things, just little things with great love." God is so good, I love to bake, and so he made all things work for the good of all for those three days.

The recreation of Esther's story enthralled me. There was no way I could fail to see God's hand in all this. Had I read about Esther in the Bible, it would not have made sense to me. But the manner in which it was presented on that stage intrigued me and piqued just enough interest for me to want to know more.

> And who knows but that you have come to the royal position for such a time as this?
>
> Esther 4:14 (NIV)

I had a nagging feeling that somewhere in that verse was a meaning far deeper, and it was meant for me to search for it. As a new Christian, I feared being too bold to think that a story in the Bible could have a direct meaning in my own personal life. And, heaven forbid, I ever think there could be any similarity between myself and a queen.

Over the course of the next several months, the story of Esther would serve as my first lesson to an awareness of how God can use people like me. That was a lightning bolt moment!

Esther's preparation had begun many years before she even went to live with Mordecai. But even more preparation was needed before she would be brought to the king. It was considered quite an honor to be presented to the king.

She was cloistered away from family and friends and all that was familiar to her. It was a long period of aloneness.

When I think back to how many years it had been since I had become a nurse and my years working in the operating room that prepared me to care for Patrick, I find it so interesting to see the curves drawing closer to becoming a circle.

I certainly felt cloistered away from my friends and my support group for the months I was caring for Patrick.

But what an honor it was to care for one's brother and a man of God.

I could look back over the past three decades and see how the Lord had begun my preparation for such a time as this. And no matter how many detours or side trips I chose, I could not thwart his plans.

I was at Patrick's side because thirty-some years ago, God had nudged my nursing career into one area, the operating room. God had qualified me to step into a very delicate situation and do what had to be done for my brother.

It was becoming clearer now why the Lord had kept me alive. It was all part of his very integral and intimate plan for me.

> You did not choose me, but I chose you.
>
> John 15:16 (NIV)

The retreat was a real "high," but now it was back to work and reality. No one could understand my hurt, and no one could accompany me. This time of existential loneliness left me feeling abandoned, lost, and empty. I had been interacting with the Thursday Life Group. I had been reading my devotionals every morning. I wanted answers, not another bus trip or a night with friends. Where was that secret place? I wanted to feel the vibrations in my soul again.

"Lord, I've been raised Catholic. We believed because that's what we were taught to do. I love what my sisters in Christ are showing me. I want to be like them. I envy their knowledge and unquestionable trust, but most of all, the closeness and relationship I see they have with you," I cried out.

In one of Thomas Merton's selected writings, he describes the moment when the first chirps of the waking day birds mark the *point vierge* of the dawn under a sky as yet without real light, a moment of awe and inexpressible innocence, when the Father in perfect *silence* opens their eyes.

They begin to speak to him, not with fluent song but with an awakening question that is their dawn state, their state at the *point vierge*. Their condition asks if it is time for them to *be*. He answers *yes*. Then they, one by one, wake up and become birds. They manifest themselves as birds, beginning to sing. Presently, they will be fully themselves and will even fly (*Merton: The True Solitude,* Kansas City, MO.: Hallmark Cards Inc., 1969, p. 21).

My first chirps were "point complaints." Why did I continue this endless search and self-torment? He would open my eyes in perfect *silence*. I did not have to be fluent or eloquent. A simple, *Thank you, Lord, for this day.*

Stop looking for the elusive butterfly. Stop trying to capture rainbows. Stop trying to grasp what will never be. Wow! I did not have to trek across Tibet. In fact, I did not have to go outside my door. God would come to me. The most wonderful moment of the day is when creation in its innocence asks permission to *be* once again, as it did on the first morning that ever was. I just had to be, to let go and let him direct my path, and he would take me under his wings, and together, we would fly.

The following morning, he opened my eyes and whispered, "Call Judy. It's her birthday."

Judy and I were high school friends. We had been close friends for some forty years. She was Eric's god-mother. It had been six months since we last spoke.

"Hi, Judy. It's Roni. Happy birthday."

We chatted for more than an hour. Just as we were about to hang up, she asked, "What are you doing for Christmas?"

"I honestly don't know," I said.

"Why don't you come here for the holidays?"

"I'd love to," I said.

For years, we talked about getting together, but with her living in North Carolina and me in California, it had never happened. Just thinking about the train ride, seeing Judy and being on a real farm for the holidays helped me to step down from the tightrope. My heart immediately blossomed with a whole new attitude. It eliminated the balancing act and any concern I had about spending or not spending Christmas with my son.

It was as though God had put a shining star over North Carolina that led me to the very place he wanted me to be for the celebration of his son's birthday. Judy and I had eight days just to kick back and reminisce about all the fun things we did in our younger years. We recalled our first vacation together at the beach in Wildwood, working together at the phone company, the years we had our weekly Canasta group, the guys we dated, and our upcoming fortieth class reunion. We talked about their move to North Carolina and redoing the farm house. We discussed how God had blessed each of us with two wonderful sons.

I had a great time talking with Raymond, her older son. I left North Carolina far more enlightened through his knowledge of the Bible and the things he shared and explained.

Christmas Eve, Judy made homemade mushroom soup, along with cheese and potato pierogies, sautéed onions, and sour cream. The Christmas tree stood tall in her farm house kitchen with twinkling lights strung throughout the room. Every ornament had a story. The fireplace filled the rooms with added warmth.

A few hours later, we left to attend a service at Judy's church. What a moving and peace-filled scene to be with a friend of forty-two years listening to a beautiful message about Jesus's birth!

At the conclusion of the service, the entire congregation sang "Silent Night" as we all walked out of church, each person carrying a flickering candle. As the song ended, a gust of wind swept through, extinguishing the candles. God was there in our midst, and we could feel his presence. It still remains to me a night like none other, with memories I hold dear to my heart. I embrace it with renewed awe, knowing it was the breath of God that blew out each candle.

Every day, I took a walk through the woods and down to the pond where more memories were triggered. Twenty-two years prior, my husband and I, along with our two sons, had visited Judy and Ray. That would be our last trip to North Carolina, as we moved to California the following year. It would be the last time for all of us to be together as families. Brad and I had long since parted, and Judy and Ray were now divorced. It seemed like only yesterday I was diving off the pier into that lake. All the bittersweet memories! How does one compare a family visit to this new experience, especially now seeing Judy's two sons as Christians?

Christmas day had a special touch as we woke to the sound of the roosters crowing and the chickens clucking. The fireplace was spitting out its warmth. I caught the aromas of the honey-baked ham in the oven along with the sweet potatoes and other special trimmings. Judy had made an apple crisp. I, of course, brought homemade cookies.

I felt warmth engulf me far beyond that fireplace. There was no doubting the Lord had hand-picked this place where I would find solitude and silence, but more importantly, I would feel safe in his sanctuary.

The prophecy of his birth had been fulfilled after two thousand years, and now another prophecy had been fulfilled. He knew this day would come when I would need his guidance. He had taken all my worries away, as well as my entertainment—no television, no computer, and no phone. Just the blessing of time alone with a special friend!

For one week, Judy and I were fifteen years old again, without a care in the world as he watched over us.

A few days later, Judy's friend Lydia joined us as we drove into Durham to enjoy a wonderful lunch at a Mexican restaurant. My favorite food and my favorite thing to do, fellowship! How blessed could one person be? Lydia gave me a beautiful scroll she had printed on her computer. *Good Morning! This is God. I will be handling all of your problems today. I will not need your help. So, relax and have a great day.*

I framed that message, and to this day, it remains hanging over my computer.

On the way home, we stopped at a used bookstore. It would not be long before I realized what a treasure I had found on the shelves in that store. A resolve would be unearthed, and my life would be forever changed.

The eight days flew by, and I was on the train returning home. Two stops before the train reached Metro Park Station, I felt certain that I had found the one answer that would put an end to my many months of self-torment.

Raymond, Judy's son, had given me a book, *The Plan*, written by the evangelist Pat Robertson. I had been reading it intently during the ten-hour train ride, when I came to the part where he mentioned a little book by Mother Basilea entitled *The Hidden Treasure in Suffering*. In it, she writes "that of all the suffering we can endure, slander is the worst. It is worse than physical suffering because it cuts to the spirit and leaves lasting spiritual scars." She also states, "It is possible to get over a beating, but how does a person get over the loss of his reputation?" She goes on to say, "…that these wounds are from the hand of a loving father who would make you more like his son. Don't try to fight against them with the means of your old carnal self. Rather, receive them as a blessing from God."

Pat Robertson explains that, after he read this, he knew this was the evidence that God's spirit had rested upon him. "I was free, with a deeper anointing of God's spirit than I had ever known." He went on to say, "Instead of wanting to fight the ones who had mistreated me, I needed to thank them. They were God's instruments to lead me to a higher understanding of his love and power."

The tears welled up, and I wanted to leap up from my seat and shout, "Thank you, God!" I knew I would finally be able to go home and sleep in peace. I had said the same thing to myself many times; I wished I had been physically beaten. I knew I could have recovered from that, but I just could not get past the mental anguish and the need to know what drove my mother to want to hurt me so badly. Accepting what she had done to me was difficult enough, but the chain of events that followed and the separation from my son as a result of my mother's lies was something I didn't think I'd ever recover from.

Yet I knew it was all this pain, along with the fact that the family did not want anything to do with me, that resulted in my getting down on my knees. I knew God's presence in a way that I never dreamed possible. Any amount of suffering would be worth it, if it made me more like his son.

CODEPENDENCY AND SILENT RETREAT

I had been home only two days when the bitterness began to well up in me *again*. I recalled the closeness I had once shared with my brothers. The holidays were over, and I hadn't heard from either one.

On New Year's Eve, I went to an AA dinner dance. It was bitterly cold, and with all the hoop-la about the millennium, I wanted to get home and into my nice warm pajamas to watch the ball come down in Times Square. The whole world was feeling the anxiety, wondering if we would be thrust into darkness at midnight.

When midnight ended, we still had electricity, and all the lights were burning brightly. Even my computer had adjusted to the new date. I felt a rush of excitement thinking, *Wow, it's really the year* 2000.

The "Wow" lasted until I woke up the following morning and realized nothing had changed. The harder I tried to focus on the Lord, the more troubled I became.

My mind revisited all the times I had traded living my life for pleasing my mother, and of course, that just validated my right to feel sorry for myself. *Why? Why? Why?*

This constant roller coaster of emotions was exhausting. I wanted five minutes, that's all, just five minutes free from my own mind. I thought about quitting my job. I thought about moving back to California. But what good would changing my location do? The PA system in my mind would arrive ahead of me, just so it could greet me. Before I even got out of bed in the morning, my mind was already up chastising me. But clearly, God had not rescued me from alcohol and death just so I could lose my mind four years later.

A few days later, I received a call that would rock my world and force me to confront another devastating revelation.

"Hi, Roni, how about coming over for dinner on your birthday?" Claire asked.

"I'd love to."

Claire and Gary were part of the Life Group. All three of us were new to the church, to each other, and to Christ. We spent many hours together discussing our joys, our problems, and our excitement of this new life. Claire was one of the few people who knew my whole story. I cherished her friendship and the sincerity of her concern. Simply put, Claire was always there for me.

Claire had made a wonderful dinner and had purchased a delicious cake. Thank goodness she hadn't put candles on it. Surely they would have set off the smoke detector. We had a very pleasant dinner. Afterwards Gary went into the living room to watch television.

Claire and I remained sitting at the table, and as always I delved into my pity-pot and started describing all the details of what had been going on since the new year began. And how I just couldn't understand why my son was behaving the way he was. We were well into the third week of January, and I hadn't seen him since my mother's funeral five months prior. I hadn't really spoken to him other than the call telling me they would be busy on Thanksgiving.

I had called him in the early part of December to tell him my plans to go to North Carolina for the holidays. I had e-mailed him Judy's phone number, assuming he would call me Christmas Day. I never did hear from him. Chad called me.

"Roni, you keep expecting other people to think as you do," Claire said. "I have a wonderful book about codependency. It's a Christian study guide with stories and Bible scriptures showing the behaviors of codependents."

"Claire, with all the problems I've had throughout the years, believe me, codependency is not one of them," I replied rather defensively. "I've been on my own for so many years, I don't ask for anything and I don't depend on anyone."

"Do me a favor, Roni. Just take the book home and read it," she insisted. "This isn't about codependency as we think of it; it's more like reversed dependency. The best part is it's a Serendipity Support Group Series. It's a study guide, not just another book about codependency."

I didn't run home enthusiastically and start reading it. I was sure there would be nothing in it that would apply to my situation.

I must have had the book for about a month before I did start skimming through the pages. I began by reading the parts Claire had highlighted for herself. Everything I was reading really piqued my interest. In a matter of days that book held me hostage. My name could have been inserted in every definition and description of a codependent.

> Codependency is a form of addiction. Other people become their drug of choice. Caring for and pleasing another person or persons becomes the center of the codependent's life. They nourish others, serve others, and will sacrifice themselves for the sake of others. It is almost as if they cannot resist. They help other people whether those people want help or not. They learn to anticipate the wants, needs, and desires of others. They often find themselves doing what they really don't want to do simply because they cannot bring themselves to refuse a request. Feeling unloved, they try to earn the love of others by doing things for them *(Peace:* Richard Peace, *Codependency/Breaking Free of Entangled Relationships.* 1991 Serendipity Support Group Series, Serendipity, P.O. Box 1012, Littleton, Colorado 80160).

I wanted to jump for joy at this revelation, which eclipsed everything else I had experienced. Finally, something concrete! At the same time, I wanted to weep at having to face the sad truth of what my codependency and addictive personality had caused.

Throughout the years, I'd let it invade and intrude on my everyday existence. I had never heard the words "I love you" from either parent. I had never been hugged by either parent. The only person I knew for sure had always loved me was my husband, Brad.

Stepping out of myself and watching the memories of how I belittled him and made impossible demands on him wrenched at my insides. I had stood at an altar and vowed to love him and to honor him until death do us part, but twenty years later, I let my need for approval and love from everyone else tear us asunder.

> With no sense of self-worth, codependents often neglect themselves. "Why bother, I'm not worth it." They ignore their legitimate needs, and never take vacations, because they don't think they deserve time off. They neglect their medical and dental needs. In severe cases, this low self worth can lead to addiction, or even to suicide.
>
> —*Peace:* Richard Peace, *Codependency/Breaking Free of Entangled Relationships.* 1991 Serendipity Support Group Series, Serendipity, P.O. Box 1012, Littleton, Colorado 80160

I could have been the poster child for codependency. All five applied to me. Admitting this was more painful than writing about my incarceration. Upon my release from prison, it had been mandated by the parole board that I attend codependency meetings every week and have a card signed, showing the dates I had attended.

It was evident that all the charges against me had stemmed from my obsessive feeling of responsibility for everything and my compulsive need to make everything right.

Had the world suddenly tilted? Could my thinking be that much out of the norm? I stole money. I forged checks. I forged credit card applications. I even stole a car. It was my responsibility to do whatever was necessary to keep my sons out of foster homes. It was my responsibility to find a way to pay for Chad's medical expenses. Now fifteen years later, I was banished to the curb for my *honest* actions and my genuine concern that benefited everyone but me.

I had spent time in prison. I had uprooted my life and moved three thousand miles to help Patrick, my father, and my mother. I would have jumped in front of an oncoming locomotive to protect my sons. I had defended my brother Dennis and agreed to let him come live with us. These were just a few of the sacrifices I had made without having a clue anything was wrong.

I was stuck with one thought: "Codependents do all these things without even being asked." How sad to be forced to confront the truth. No one had asked me to come back and take care of Patrick. No one had asked me to move back to New Jersey. No one had even asked for my help. I was the one who initiated the offer in every situation.

"Roni, wait until you see how hard it is to change this behavior," Claire said.

"Oh, come on, Claire, how hard could it be?"

I had made my own choices. I could no longer pretend to understand the thought processes of other people. I was weary of trying. I knew the need to blame everyone else for my problems had to end. I knew this called for drastic changes. I could not continue living like this and harboring so many resentments.

> When his father-in-law saw all that Moses was doing for the people, he said, "What is this you are doing for the people? Why do you alone sit as judge, while all these people stand around you from morning till evening?"
>
> Exodus 18:14

Moses answered him, "Because the people come to me to seek God's will. Whenever they have a dispute, it is brought to me, and I decide between the parties and inform them of God's decrees and laws."

Exodus 18:15

Moses's father-in-law (Jethro) replied, "What you are doing is not good. You and these people who come to you will only wear yourselves out. The work is too heavy for you; you cannot handle it alone."

Exodus 18:17–18

Where was my Jethro to instruct me? Where was Jethro when I needed someone to tell me the Lord never intended for me to do all these things I was doing alone?

Claire was one hundred percent right. It was not easy to embark on another journey into uncharted waters at my age. At the same time, I felt a sense of calm and peace. Alcoholics Anonymous had taught me that I could not change anyone else; neither was it my responsibility to change anyone else. I could only change myself, persevere in the face of uncertainty, and pray I would not fall into the temptation to be the good old "jolly jump-up" who would immediately say, "Oh, I'll do it." It was AA that taught me to be honest while doing a thorough inventory of myself and to be aware of my character defects and ask God to remove them.

This was definitely an "aha" moment. A very real revelation for me. I began to take note of the many times I would offer to do things without being asked for help. It was really hard for me to pull back and resist that urge or need to offer my assistance, but little by little I was beginning to recognize that in most cases the reason I was doing this was for my own self-gratification. It's an amazing phenomenon.

I know many people think of themselves as being people pleasers, and they may very well be. But codependency is as different from people pleasing as night is from day. It's one thing to bake a cake you know someone will enjoy. But it's a far different experience when you've been told in advance that they don't need you to bake a cake, but you do it anyway. And the saddest part is doing it when you can't afford to. It's a whole different ballgame.

Thomas Merton suggested, "We become conscious that the person we think we are, here and now, is at best, an impostor and a stranger. We must constantly question his motives and penetrate his disguises."

Will the real Roni please stand up? The time had arrived for me to become friends with the stranger I had mistreated for so many years. Then I had to begin my new journey to become the woman Christ intended for me to be.

"It's Connie," said the voice on the phone. "I got a brochure in the mail for a nearby retreat. Would you like to go?"

"You know me, I'm game for it."

"I have to be honest. It will be quite different from the one this past October. This is a silent retreat."

"What does that mean?" I asked, cautiously.

"When we arrive Friday, we'll all have dinner together, followed by a meeting and fellowship. After that, the entire weekend is one of silence, except for lectures on Saturday morning and afternoon."

"What about mealtimes?"

"Even then, there is no talking."

"Oh my goodness! I can't picture me, the chatterbox, being still for an entire weekend."

We both laughed over that.

"I've been on this retreat twice, and it's a wonderful experience. Most of the women who attend are from AA, but it's not an AA retreat. It's more of a spiritual retreat. It's held at a convent, and the nuns do the cooking. It's awesome."

"Okay, let's do it. What a wonderful prelude this will be before we leave for Israel next month."

Although I agreed to go, I had misgivings. Anyone would have thought I'd been asked to lie on a bed of nails. How would I occupy my time? Connie told me we would each have our own bedroom. What if I got bored? My nervousness commingled with excitement. I packed up eight meditation cassettes, my Walkman, and one book. I had enough to keep me occupied between the lectures and mealtimes.

After our Friday evening dinner, we all met in a cozy room with a fireplace that looked much like a library. Grace, the woman who had organized the retreat, welcomed us and explained the agenda for the following two days.

We took a ten-minute break, at which time Grace asked if I would be willing to give a brief talk about my experience in recovery. Little did Connie and I know that we had both been asked. It was funny.

"I have chosen two women for tonight's get-acquainted gathering. They will tell us a little about their background and share their experience, strength, and hope. Roni will be our first speaker, and Connie will be next. Connie has attended this retreat before. This is Roni's first time with us. So let's give them both a welcome round of applause."

With that introduction, I got up to speak. I had twenty minutes to get it out before I had to zip it up. I thought that was quite humorous.

The weekend would come to remind me of the time during which Brad and I began dating. We spoke little. Just being with one another was enough. We felt comfortable sharing our secret thoughts and dreams.

Saturday morning, we met in the chapel for a service. Brother Jason had chosen special scriptures for us to read. Chapels have always been a place of tranquility where my spirits are refreshed. I left feeling lighter, knowing the Lord had lifted my burdens. I wanted more of that quiet time in the chapel with the stained-glass windows.

Following the service, we quietly joined in the dining room for breakfast. One by one, as we finished eating, we stacked our dirty dishes on the trays. The sound of the music wafted through the halls making for a wonderful transition as we entered the library.

Brother Jason gave a wonderful talk about the need for silence and time alone with God. His lecture was inspiring and motivated me to return to my room in silent contemplation.

Later, I realized that God had given me time to be with him in silence. It was an opportunity to reflect on the past eight months. I wasn't ready to enter a convent or become a nun. However, I became immersed in gratitude for my freedom. I could go outside for a walk, listen to music, or just lie down. This was a time of sacred silence as I contrasted the clanging of the cell doors and shouting of fellow prisoners ten years earlier. There were no distractions here, just thirty-six hours of silently waiting in his presence.

> Be still, and know that I am God.
>
> Psalm 46:10 (NIV)

At noon, we met for lunch. That was followed by another lecture. I returned to my room with a determination to be still and listen. It's difficult to keep eyes open when I'm so relaxed. I lay on the bed and listened to a few meditation cassettes and fell asleep. I woke feeling refreshed, and I read over my notes from the lecture. I wanted the clock to stop ticking so I could lavish in this peace and quiet. I was alone with God, to weep and cry out for his guidance and comfort during this difficult time of change in my life.

There was no lecture after dinner, so I decided to spend the evening reading.

During my recent visit with Judy in North Carolina, we had gone to a used bookstore. As I was browsing, my attention had been drawn to one book, even though it hadn't been particularly flashy in appearance. However, it was slightly out of alignment with the rest of the books on the shelf. *The Book of Job* by Thomas Moore called out to me, "Take me home."

As I sat by the window in my room that evening at the retreat, I skimmed through a few pages. Just as the book had stood out on the shelf, there were two verses that jumped off the page at me.

> Then Job answered the Lord: "I am unworthy—how can I reply to you? I put my hand over my mouth."
>
> Job 40:3, 4 (NIV)

My heart skipped a beat. I could barely contain myself long enough to remain in my room until the following morning. The thought of Job putting his hand over his mouth captivated me. The visual picture made it clear and simple. Job was suddenly confronted with the reality that the Lord spoke to him, and he knew immediately he was not equipped to answer.

I was the female counterpart of Job, and I could feel God's presence in that room with me. I had always been the one who had something to say about everything. I was the Doubting Thomas who questioned everything. Suddenly, I was silenced. At the same moment, I felt a leap of excitement.

Have you ever seen a fifty-seven-year-old cheerleader? Neither have I! But I sure felt like one at that moment. All that was missing were the pom-poms. I was on fire for the Lord after reading those verses, and I knew immediately they would transform my life.

"Rah, Rah, I found a secret! Rah, Rah, I found Job! I found an ally! I found someone whose erratic outbursts matched my own." I fought to contain myself as I continued to cheer in silence.

Sunday, we met in the chapel for another service. The silence and service ended simultaneously. The music continued to waft through the halls as we rejoiced in a wonderful celebration breakfast.

As we were about to leave, the nuns gave each of us a bag of apples from their orchard, and tucked inside was the recipe for their apple crisp. They knew from past retreats that their apple crisp was a hit. We had had it for dessert both evenings, and it was scrumptious. It made for a very happy ending to a most inspiring and memorable weekend.

I could not get home fast enough to delve into the buried treasures I knew were in *The Book of Job*. My life was about to change once *again*—but this time for the good.

Do not conform any longer to the pattern of the world, but be transformed by the renewing of your mind.

Romans 12:2 (NIV)

LESSONS FROM JOB

> In all this, Job did not sin by charging God with wrongdoing.
>
> Job 1:22 (NIV)

I had often heard people use the phrase, "Oh, he or she has the patience of Job" (pronounced Jobe). However, I never had a clue who or what Job was or its relationship to patience.

I had heard the pastor refer to Job in one of his sermons. So Job was a person in the Bible. I read the book of Job in its entirety, understanding none of it. I reread it and still could not see any connection between Job and patience. Yet I was fascinated by him.

It begins with a commentary by the author. Thomas Moore refers to the book of Job as a true comic jewel and goes so far as to say that a good dramatist could present Job in all its dark humor and stinging irony.

Reaching page nine, I knew God was speaking to me. Not audibly, but his message was loud and clear.

To date, no one knows who actually wrote the book of Job in the Bible. Whether it's truth, half-truth, fact, fiction, poetry, myth, folklore, or riddle is irrelevant. What is significant is the profound impact it had on me. It captivated me and enthralled me.

Three years later, it continued to pierce my very soul. I found some deeply disturbing similarities and just as many differences between Job's life and my own.

In the end, it would penetrate into my most disheartening situation. It would help in my search for an answer to my own personal enigma. It would bring me a peace I never dreamed possible and take me to heights I did not know existed. It turned my world upside down, and for the first time, my feet were planted on the ground.

In essence, it is about the hardships and disease that befall Job and his endurance and faith without any knowledge of a prior arrangement made between God and Satan.

The Lord declares Job to be a self-righteous person, blameless and sinless. He knows that whatever Satan does, Job will remain faithful. Job was well-known and respected for his integrity, honesty, and generosity.

When a messenger came to deliver the news to Job that his children were all dead, Job fell to the ground and worshipped.

> Naked I came from my mother's womb, and naked I will depart. The Lord gave and the Lord has taken away; may the name of the Lord be praised.
>
> Job 1:21 (NIV)

Wow! The ultimate generosity and the ultimate poverty when the giver becomes the gift.

Why do you complain to him that he answers none of man's words?

Job 33:13 (NIV)

The same questions that were asked during Job's time are being asked today. The same accusations that were made then are being made today.

I had a revelation. What if I were to stop asking, "Why?" On a conscious level, would I be capable of putting the brakes on, whenever that one particular question came into my mind? Yes! Was I ready to accept that I would never find all the answers? Yes! Could I remove that one word from my vocabulary? Yes! Could it be that simple? Yes!

In one part of his commentary, Moore summed up nine months worth of my thoughts very eloquently and simply. He said:

> After working as a psychotherapist for twenty years and sitting hour after hour with people, I came to one conclusion. People want a reason for why they are suffering. If they could find an answer, they believe their suffering would be relieved, as if by magic. Or at least it would become bearable. In other words, if suffering made sense, they believed they could endure it.

Moore said he could recall many hours of therapy during which a patient would present an explanation for "why" he or she was suffering. By the end of the hour, the explanation had been discussed quite thoroughly, but it still left the person feeling empty and unresolved.

The following week, the patient would present an altogether new explanation with fresh enthusiasm and hope, only to find the familiar emptiness and dissatisfaction at the end of the session.

This was the type of situation I was experiencing. Unfortunately, for me it wasn't a weekly occurrence; it was happening hourly. I would analyze the entire scenario and replay it over and over in my head. Sensing I had reached a satisfactory conclusion, I would discuss it with a friend. An hour later, a new piece of the puzzle came into play changing everything and leaving me even more depressed. This forced me into rethinking everything over again. I rationalized this new scenario feeling certain this would be the final answer. Ten minutes later, it changed.

Someone once said: *Too much thinking can bring a man to distraction and distraction to ruin.* My thinking had put me on a collision course headed toward self-destruction; still I could not stop it. The more I tried pulling in the reins, the more the thoughts persisted. My imagination played even more havoc. The obsessive and compulsive need to know why my mother kicked me out became my straightjacket.

I just could not come to terms with how easily my family could dispense of me as if I never existed.

It is truly incredible how many thoughts can go through the human mind within a fifteen-minute period. We can tear down a whole city and rebuild it. The list of scenarios and projections is truly endless. It reminds me of a Rubik's Cube. No matter how many ways you twist and turn it, very few people can figure it out. With the mind, it's impossible to get the right combination when you're dealing with so many people and their diverse perceptions.

We could spend a lifetime explaining ourselves, and it's not going to change the other person's thinking if they have not shared your experience in precisely the same way.

Recalling Todd, my brother, standing in the pulpit giving the eulogy at my mother's funeral, I had to wonder, *Who was he talking about?* With the wheels still grinding, I thought, *Wouldn't it be interesting to strip away the pretense and lies and listen to a eulogy from each child. The listeners would swear we were talking about three different mothers.* He had moved away thirty years ago. And during that entire time, he only came east one weekend a year. He would *drop in* and stay overnight, but only because he had business in New York. So what did he know?

"If the doors of perception were cleansed," wrote Blake, "man would see everything as it is, infinite."

The year I moved back to New Jersey, Todd had traveled one million miles on United Airlines. Traveling was the main function of his livelihood. My mother was so proud of him. At her wake, Todd wore a tie with airplanes on it, and he let everyone know his mother had given it to him.

Ironically, I had shopped for it, paid for it, and sent it to him. I had enclosed a card, *Love, Mom.* It's an arresting observation to see the truth of how "a man thinketh in his heart." Todd believed in his heart that the tie came from his mother; therefore, he wore it proudly. We can only imagine where that tie would be had he known *dear sis* sent it.

I have this vision of God looking down and laughing. There is no way for us to know what another person is thinking. Every day, we have visible and invisible experiences that, at one moment, can help us or another moment, hurt us.

Truth, after all, is ultimately known only by God. He *alone* has the ability to see into our hearts and know everything involved in any situation and relationship.

Phillip Keller, in his book, *A Shepherd Looks at Psalm 23*, wrote the following:

> Human beings, being what they are, somehow feel entitled to question the reasons for everything that happens to them. In many instances, life itself becomes a continuous criticism and dissection of one's circumstances and acquaintances. We are often quick to forget our blessings, slow to forget our misfortunes.

I could not rest with this tug-of-war going on in my head, but hearing that word, *dissection*, really gave me a start. I had dissected just about every action and comment that had been made since I moved back.

It was not the act of her kicking me out or leaving me homeless that was still holding me in this freeze-frame. It was the psychological aspect of it. The plotting and scheming and drawing my own sons into her deviousness. It was that need to know *why* my mother did this to me that was so devastating. What had I done to her?

I would never find the one answer that would satisfy me, simply because there was no answer. It happened. I needed to move on. I cannot tell you what an awesome revelation this was for me. Putting it into practice was miraculous. If I continued in my pursuit to know *why*, I would end up with a thousand different opinions from a thousand different people.

It was time for me to start over again, and the only place I would find some peace and order was in God's will. "We are quick to forget our blessings, slow to forget our misfortunes." Keller's words were right!

You cannot read through Job without seeing the absurdity. The friends he thinks he can rely on to comfort him turn out to be his worst tormentors. The more I read, the more comical it became. Suddenly, I started to see the similarities when one of his friends dared him to utter his innocence. One question in particular came immediately to mind.

"Are you trying to tell me Grandma is lying?" asked my son. He did exactly what Job's tormentors had done. Eric was daring me to utter my innocence against my mother's infallibility.

Job's friends had no doubt he was a sinner and a liar and that's why terrible things happened to him. It's intriguing to watch people venture into situations they have no business being part of, and it's riveting to listen to their opinionated summations of events they know nothing about. They barely saw the flames, never felt the heat, and yet they could describe every detail of the fire.

The story of Job is the eighteenth book in the Old Testament, written well over two thousand years ago; and today, those dialogues and conversations mirror my own to a chilling and thought-provoking degree. However, there is one major difference: most of my dialogue and conversations were one-sided. All my screaming, yelling, questioning, accusing, blaming, and crying took place in the privacy of my own mind.

Samuel Beckett wrote a play titled *Waiting For Godot*. In it, two men stand on an empty stage, hands in their pockets, staring at each other. No action, no plot, they just stand there waiting for Godot. But who is Godot? Is he a person? Does he represent God?

Christian author Lewis Smedes suggests Godot "stands for the pipe dreams that a lot of people hang on to as an escape." At the end of the play, they are still waiting.

When the fiftieth anniversary of that play was celebrated, someone asked Beckett, "Now, will you tell us who Godot is?"

He answered, "How should I know?"

The probability of a play without a plot, just two men standing on a stage through the entire ninety minutes, reaching a fiftieth anniversary, in my opinion, is impossible. The fact that it did really should not have surprised me. I had been *waiting* for my mother to tell me she loved me for fifty-five years. Not only had I wasted a whole lifetime, I had become so desperate to be loved that I destroyed my life in seeking that love.

It's a parable of many of our lives—empty and meaningless, a pointless matter of waiting. We all have our Godots.

My Godots were my expectations. Expecting to find that one answer to my one question, "Why?" Expecting my family to show some concern. Expecting my mother to love me. Expecting her to tell me she was sorry. Then expecting her to ask me to move back in with her. My list of expectations, endless!

We fool ourselves into thinking that, if we dig deep enough, something hidden will be revealed, and *poof,* the magic genie will appear, giving us the one answer that will satisfy us.

Meanwhile, we stand on the empty stage waiting.

> Brace yourself like a man; I will question you, and you shall answer me.
>
> Job 38:3 (NIV)

God never attempts to explain himself to Job. He doesn't tell Job why all the calamity happened to him. He makes it very clear that he will be the one to ask the questions and Job will be the one to answer, not the other way around.

God is God. He doesn't answer to us. Yet we continue to question him, "Why me, God?"

Imagine our temerity and boldness to think we have the right to question God. We are questioning the very person who has created the oceans whose waves have never ceased to come and go and halt at the same place every day.

> "This far you may come and no farther; here is where your proud waves halt."
>
> Job 38:11 (NIV)

Every year brings the different seasons, and all of creation moves in perfect harmony. Who amongst us has ever seen a springtime that has failed to bring forth leaves on the trees and buds on the rosebushes? In autumn, have the leaves ever failed to slowly and miraculously turn from green to red to orange to yellow before they flutter to the ground? Can any of us say there was no winter last year or no summer the year before?

I have lived through more than fifty winters and fifty summers without ever thinking there may not be a summer next year. Hundreds of people plan all winter for their summer vacation. They never think, *We better wait and see if there will be a summer.* It is a given! God's love is a given and his love is consistent—as consistent as the summer and winter!

We are inquisitive by nature, and it's not easy reconditioning ourselves to stop asking why. It takes time. But I assure you, it is worth it. The peace of mind I have today cannot be compared to anything on this earth. The cross-examining, the inquiring, the searching, and the prying have stopped. The years I wasted seeking answers have become hours I spend with the Lord and reading his Word, time looking forward to enjoying a peace-filled life. The riches are beyond comprehension.

> Do you know how the clouds hang poised, those wonders of him who is perfect in knowledge?
>
> Job 37:15 (NIV)

Phillip Keller notes the following:

> I meditate on Psalm 23 and frequently go out at night to walk alone under the stars and remind myself of His majesty and might. Looking up at the star-studded sky, I remember that at least 250,000,000 x 250,000,000 such bodies—each larger than our sun, have been scattered across the vast spaces of the universe by His hand.

My mind cannot absorb that. No words can describe the enormity of that concept.

> Lift your eyes and look to the heavens: Who created all these? He who brings out the starry host one by one, and calls them each by name. Because of his great power and mighty strength, not one of them is missing.
>
> Isaiah 40:26 (NIV)

And I, Veronika, assumed I had the right to question this very same God who created the heavens and the earth, along with the arrogance to think he should give an account to me.

> The secret things belong to the Lord our God.
>
> Deuteronomy 29:29 (NIV)

Today, I relish in the sentiment of knowing God has secrets and he has surprises and they are all for my good. There is nothing I need to think about or worry about. God has it covered. My only job is to keep focused on where he is leading me. God is no longer just a conscious thought. He is my conscience!

> Is not your wickedness great? Are not your sins endless?
>
> Job 22:5 (NIV)

Job did not allow his friends to convince him that their accusations were true. He knew he was a good person and a generous one.

That's almost unprecedented in today's world. People are obsessed with a need to be liked by everyone. Many drug addicts and alcoholics display two very destructive characteristics: low self-esteem and a need to please in order to be accepted and loved, in most cases, by their families. Many of us could change the words self-esteem to other-esteem, because our concern is always based on what other people think of us.

Very few people could stand up to the taunting and ridicule that Job experienced. Not once did Job respond by saying, "Yeah, you guys are probably right." He stood up to them and made a firm declaration.

> Have I not wept for those in trouble? Has not my soul grieved for the poor?
>
> Job 30:25 (NIV)

Still they continued to make accusations against him and taunt him. But the only person who mattered to Job was God. He needed to speak to God to be assured by him that what he had done was good. He didn't care what anyone else thought.

I was eyes to the blind and feet to the lame.

Job 29:15 (NIV)

I had been eyes for my mother and feet for my brother. But like Job's friends, my family could not remember the good things I had done.

I had the good fortune to hear Loughlan Sofield give a lecture on self-esteem and Christian growth. He said, "The love of God begins and ends with the love of oneself."

I so desperately wanted to love God with all of my being, but loving myself? How could I do that after all the years of rejection and criticism?

Sofield continued:

> As Christians we are always called to growth, we are not called to survival. That's what God wants of us. In order to grow, we must have our basic human needs met. We have the need to feel safe and secure … to belong, to be loved; we also have the need for self-esteem, to value ourselves, to feel as though in our own hearts we are people who matter.

Upon hearing this, was it any wonder I couldn't love myself? None of these needs had ever been met. I had lived my entire life just trying to survive. I had never even considered growth.

Sofield said, "It's possible to have high self-esteem in one area and low self-esteem in another." The example he gave could have been me. A woman he knew was a high school principal. She knew she did a good job; she knew she was competent and professional.

On the flip-side, she was the daughter of parents who had a lot of expectations of her. They recently moved nearby and were calling her constantly to come over to repair things, to shop for them, and they expected her to be there. Even though she, herself, was an adult, had her own family, and needed to be back at school, she continued to look at their expectations of her and think badly of herself, *I'm not a good daughter.*

I had a very demanding job in the medical field, and I was knowledgeable and competent. The manner in which I handled my mother's medical needs was very professional. My self-esteem in these areas was extremely high. Yet, in the end, I allowed her to destroy whatever self-esteem I had.

Sofield goes on to say we all have this ego ideal, which is all the things we think we should be if we're going to be a good person. We grow up hearing: "You're a good girl if you do this or that; you're a bad girl if you don't do this or that." Throughout life, people have expectations of what constitutes or makes us a good person. Many of us were raised to believe we're only okay if we're perfect.

Sofield made two important points. The first was God is as present in failure as he is in success. I had not failed my mother, but even if I had, God was still present. The second was to replace the issue of perfection with "I will try." If I continue to do the best I can, I will grow to be the person God has called me to be.

For I was hungry and you gave me something to eat, I was thirsty and you gave me something to drink, I was a stranger and you invited me in. "Then the righteous will answer him, 'Lord, when did we see you hungry and feed you, or thirsty and give you something to drink? When did we see you a stranger and invite you in? When did we see you sick or in prison and go to visit you?' The King will reply, 'I tell you the truth, whatever you did for one of the least of these brothers of mine, you did for me.'"

Matthew 25:35, 37, 40 (NIV)

What better confirmation could I be given? That was my answer. I had tried. I did for my mother, my father, and my brothers just as I would have done for the Lord.

What an awesome affirmation to help us with our sense of self-esteem and to start learning how to love oneself, and then to experience truly loving God.

The simplicity of my life today is radically different from ten years ago. I've learned to trust the Lord and to believe in myself. Job taught me that obstacles come to all of us, and I'm not to question them. I face them and pray for God's guidance and strength as he walks through them with me.

I do not see my adversities as tests from God. He gave us free will, and every day we are confronted with new challenges and new experiences. When we teach our children how to ride a bike, eventually we have to let them go. And if they fall, we didn't cause it.

Similarly, God doesn't cause bad things to happen to us. The times we make wrong choices and fall, God wants us to turn to him just as I wanted my son to run home to me. I wanted to be the one to comfort him, to kiss his scrapes and to put a Band-Aid on them. I did not want him going to the neighbor's house.

How could Job's friends not make any attempt to comfort him knowing he was suffering from the loss of his children along with his physical pain? Instead, they did just the opposite. They tormented him and accused him of wrongdoing and lying. But Job never stooped to the same level as his friends.

Like Job, I wanted to stand up and shout my innocence to the whole world one minute, and the next I wanted God to give me a reason why my life was in shambles.

In his book about Job, Stephen Mitchell writes:

> The same arguments are recycled again and again, with more and more stridency, until they become merely boring. Job's speeches are a kaleidoscope of conflicting emotions, addressed to his friends, to himself, to God. His attitude shifts constantly…He wants to die, he wants to prove he is innocent, he wants to shake his fist at God.

That was me in a nutshell. My thoughts and speeches were a kaleidoscope of conflicting emotions. I wanted to die. I wanted to prove my innocence. My arguments were recycled a million times until they became boring and offensive.

Why me? There is no answer because it was the wrong question.

> "My servant Job will pray for you, and I will accept his prayer and not deal with you according to your folly. You have not spoken of me what is right, as my servant Job has."

Job 42:5 (NIV)

How many times had I read through the book of Job before that verse jumped off the page with startling clarity? God knows when he tells Job to pray for his tormentors he will do as he is told, unlike me who would respond, "But that's not fair."

Nowhere in the above scripture does God ask Job if he would be willing to pray for his tormentors. Can you picture God saying, "Listen, Job, I have a request to make of you?"

Nor does he make any attempt to explain what a wonderful thing it would be for Job to pray for his tormentors.

Imagine being told to pray for the very people who claim to be your friends and care about you when all they did was torment you at the lowest point in your life. It's gut-wrenching when someone tries to load guilt and shame on you when you're going through a rough time.

For me, praying for others was extremely difficult. I had to fight every demon in me. I had to forgive my mother for all the pain her lies caused and for the separation she brought about between Eric and me. It was time to forgive the entire family and pray for them with no strings attached. I couldn't bargain, "Okay, God, I'll pray for them, if you make sure that so-and-so does this-or-that for me." This was the ultimate sacrifice of ego, victimization, pity, blame, and every other excuse I held on to.

Prayer is not an attempt to change God's mind; it's allowing God to change our mind. God wants to soften our hearts. He wants us to cooperate and follow him.

Northrop Frye describes the book of Job as comedy. He says, "If we look at the sort of characters who impede the progress of comedy, we find they are always people who are in some kind of mental bondage, who are help-lessly driven by ruling passions, neurotic compulsions, social rituals, and selfishness."

Once we grasp the full significance of the book of Job, it's easier to see the parallel to our own lives.

When I was a child, there was no humor in my home. My parents were driven by ruling passions, mis-interpreted religious doctrine, the punishing God, social rituals, and mental bondage to their false beliefs.

Job's tormentors were led by misguided beliefs. They believed with absolute surety that Job had to have done some very vile things or else he would not have suffered such terrible losses and pain.

"The freer the society, the greater the variety of indi-viduals it can tolerate." (Shakespeare: Modern Essays in Criticism, published by Oxford University Press, Inc. 1957, *The Argument of Comedy*: Northrop Frye, pg. 82)

The above quote is the lesson I've learned through other recovering alcoholics. We, the good, the bad, the beautiful, the ugly, the old, the young, the rich, and the poor, share a common malady. We are no longer held in the clutches of alcohol, nor do social rituals drive us. That gives us a freedom that cannot be described. Through perseverance and hard work, we are able to accept life on life's terms. Each day we yield to God, and then we are able to do the same thing he told Job to do—pray for our tormentors.

In his book, *The Power of Myth*, Joseph Campbell is being interviewed by Bill Moyers.

> Moyers: "Do you ever have this sense when you are following your bliss, as I have at moments, of being helped by hidden hands?"

Campbell: "All the time. It is miraculous. If you follow your bliss, you put yourself on a kind of track that has been there all the while, waiting for you, and the life that you ought to be living is the one you are living. Follow your bliss and don't be afraid, and the doors will open where you didn't know they were going to be."

Campbell goes on to say: "When you take all the 'chances' that happen to you as if it had been of your intention—you evoke the participation of your will."

He states that by doing this, "You are not grabbed because you have released yourself from the grabbers of fear, lust, and duties."

That is acceptance! I try very hard to incorporate this thinking into my life. I look at every good turn and every wrong turn as the path I'm supposed to be on. I have been pleasantly awed at all the doors that have opened with adventures just waiting for me. There are times I don't like where the path leads me, but I am receptive of the end result, because I have the guarantee of knowing that God will work all things for the good of those who love him.

Therein lies my bliss with the help of his hidden hands. Therein lies the peace I must access in order to experience God's presence in my life.

PILGRIMAGE TO THE HOLY LAND

When Job finished praying for his friends, the Lord blessed the later part of his life.

Job 42:12 (NIV)

At fifty-seven, I began to experience God's blessings. And it had only just begun. In March of the new millennium, I boarded the plane that would take me to the Holy Land. We arrived in Tel Aviv at midnight, where our tour guide awaited us and drove our group of forty to the nearby hotel. We enjoyed a very late buffet and a restful night of sleep.

The following morning, we had breakfast and boarded the bus that would take us to Jerusalem. Halfway there, I broke down and sobbed. I could not believe that I, a sinner, was nearing the very land where my Lord and Savior had lived and died and had been raised again.

Walking on that holy ground in Jerusalem is a powerful experience that pierces you and confirms beyond any doubt that you are in a region where Jesus once walked.

We took a boat ride across the Sea of Galilee where the aura of calmness seeped through every fiber of my body. We all closed our eyes as the pastor led us in prayer. One by one, we raised our hands and sang praises to the Lord.

Later, as we sat in silence, I asked myself, *What was it like 2000 years ago? How did the apostles feel knowing they were with Jesus?* He was with them in the storm, and he calmed the sea just as he was doing in my own life. What a testimony to his faithfulness!

> Then he got up and rebuked the winds and the waves. And it was completely calm.
>
> Matthew 8:26 (NIV)

Following the boat ride, we went to a restaurant along the shoreline. One of the entrees was St. Peter's fish dinner. Connie and I were sitting with Pastor Spencer, and just as he was finishing his meal, I happened to notice something shiny reflecting on his plate. "Pastor Spencer, look inside your fish; there's a coin wedged between the bones." He thought I was joking. The restaurant had put coins in selected dinners, and Pastor Spencer happened to get a special one. We all laughed. That incident added to my growing list of memories.

> Take the first fish you catch; open its mouth and you will find a four-drachma coin. Take it and give it to them for my tax and yours.
>
> Matthew 17:27 (NIV)

It was wonderful to have three pastors with us who described all the areas and read scriptures that correlated to each place we visited. In this same area of Galilee, Jesus preached to the people and performed the miracle of the multiplication of the fishes and loaves.

The Mount of Beatitudes, where Jesus gave the Sermon on the Mount, is covered with bougainvillea and other beautiful flowers. We sat outside the church on the hillside and took turns reading the beatitudes. Visualizing Jesus preaching those words we had learned so many years ago was spellbinding. It immediately triggered the memory of the hillside I had sat on during the church camping trip eight months prior. I had tried then to capture the feel of what it had been like listening to Jesus preach. Now I was sitting on that very spot.

It's impossible to comprehend the reality of where I had been ten years prior and where the Lord had brought me at this moment. It's a profound and powerful experience. How does one describe a moment and a feeling that is almost indescribable? How does a person go from prison in 1990 to the Promised Land in 2000? I pulled a petal off one of the flowers as I said, "He loves me, He truly loves me." That petal remains in my Bible inserted on the page with the Beatitudes.

> Blessed are those who are persecuted because of righteousness, for theirs is the kingdom of heaven.
>
> Matthew 5:10 (NIV)

Another day, we visited The Cenacle, the room of the Last Supper. There are no cameras allowed. It is a room that commands complete silence with due reverence. You almost feel as though it is a place that no one should enter. I wanted to fall on my face and beg his forgiveness. I stood there in solemn awe knowing it was in this very room where Jesus took a towel and filled a basin with water and washed the feet of his apostles. There is no greater example of humility. He became the Servant. Then he shared his last meal with his twelve perfectly chosen imperfect men.

To stroll through the Garden of Gethsemane where Jesus's sweat turned to blood almost paralyzed me with awe. One tree, still standing, is believed to be the same one that was there the night Jesus prayed in the garden. The trunk of the tree is huge in circumference and very gnarled, but the branches and fullness of the leaves stand erect and magnificent. This beautiful garden holds the memory of Jesus's agony.

> Jesus fell with his face to the ground and prayed, "My Father, if it is possible, may this cup be taken from me. Yet not as I will, but as you will."
>
> Matthew 26:36 (NIV)

Walking the Via Dolorosa, "Way of the Cross," brought me back to my childhood. I had attended Catholic grammar school, and every Friday during Lent, the entire school walked over to church to hear the priest recite the Stations of the Cross. I couldn't wait for the priest to read the sixth one, "This is where Veronika wiped the face of Jesus with her veil." I now stood on that same path where the woman I was named after had soaked up the blood and sweat from Jesus's face.

Jesus's slow, agonizing trek to The Place of the Skull, Golgotha, had taken place right where I walked. We reached the platform that had been erected so visitors could see Calvary, and I tried to visualize the cross with Jesus hanging on it. The shame of my past at that moment became almost unbearable.

Sunday, the three pastors held a service in The Garden Tomb. The built-in benches throughout the garden are surrounded by hillsides with beautiful plants and flowers and paths of flagstone. We were each given a tiny wooden cup, shaped like a chalice, filled with grape juice so we could share in unity the remembrance of Jesus's blood that was shed for us.

> At the place where Jesus was crucified there was a garden, and in the garden a new tomb, in which no one had ever been laid.
>
> John 19:41 (NIV)

After the service, we strolled quietly through the garden. To step into his tomb is heart-wrenching. Nailed on the outside of the door of the tomb is a wooden plaque: *HE IS NOT HERE—HE HAS RISEN.*

My pilgrimage took place exactly forty years from the time I graduated from high school. It was clearly the end of my forty years of wandering in the desert. Now I knew how the Israelites felt as they crossed over the Jordan into the "land of milk and honey."

I could not imagine any experience more moving than the moment I was baptized in the Jordan River. I stared at the heavens saying, "My God, you have placed me in these very same waters where your own Son stood." Just then, two of the pastors placed me beneath those waters. I did not emerge the same person.

Therefore, I am now going to allure her; I will lead her into the desert and speak tenderly to her. There I will give her back her vineyards and will make the Valley of Achor (trouble) a door of hope. There she will sing (or respond) as in the days of her youth, as in the day she came up out of Egypt.

Hosea 2:14–15 (NIV)

Only in hindsight could I comprehend that with God's perfect planning comes perfect balance. No one but God could have given me fourteen of the most glorious days of my life. No one but God could have divided those fourteen days into perfectly equal parts of joy, tears, glory, grace, fun, excitement, fellowship, awe, laughter, silence, calm, love; the list goes on *ad infinitum.*

There is a time for everything, and a season for every activity under heaven: a time to weep and a time to laugh.

Ecclesiastes 3:1, 4 (NIV)

We did not just go into his tomb and cry, nor did we look at Calvary and weep then travel home in sadness thinking only of what he suffered. We were there during the celebration of Purim, where we saw kids on merry-go-rounds, eating cotton candy, laughing, and having a joyous time.

We traveled slightly ahead of the Pope's arrival. There were beautiful posters with his picture, announcing his arrival, throughout Israel. It could be no coincidence that the day I, an Irish woman, was baptized, just happened to fall on March 17, St. Patrick's Day.

The last stop on our trip was Eliat, Israel's resort, where you would swear you were in Palm Springs. It was magnificent, with its palm trees swaying over the azure blue swimming pools and the beaches of the nearby Mediterranean Sea. All of Israel was beautiful. I stood in wonder on the balcony of every hotel we stayed at and took pictures of the sunrises and sunsets. My camera was filled with snapshots of the hillsides, the poolside chats with our fellow travelers, the homes built into mountainsides, and the underwater observatory where we were the ones in the tank submerged into the world of sea creatures.

Every place, everything, and every experience filled me to overflowing with gratitude for this once-in-a-lifetime miraculous opportunity.

The last night of our stay in Eliat, several of us went out for a walk, and we could not believe the sight that stood before us. There was a little amusement park on the boardwalk that gave us the thrill and joy of watching pastors and their wives, along with several from our group, including myself and Connie, steering our bumper cars and laughing as we crashed into one another. No one could ever convince me that God does not have a sense of humor. This was more than a Kodak moment, more than a Hallmark moment; this was a God moment.

Two of the pastors who traveled with us told me the Bible would never be the same after I returned home.

It would have been very difficult for them to comprehend someone like me taking this journey, someone who had never read the Bible and knew very little about it. They had no way of knowing my entire life would take on new meaning. Nothing for me would ever be the same again. And to that I can say, Amen!

Our tour guide brought us to a jewelry outlet, and most of the women had purchased at least one item. Connie wore her gold necklace with a porcelain angel on it, and looking at it made me sad. It was a great keepsake that she would have for the rest of her life. I am not a jewelry person, so I declined everything that was shown to me. As we walked through the airport toward the terminal, I had my regrets. I was silently chastising myself for not having purchased a similar keepsake when something caught my attention. In the middle of the terminal was a glass display counter containing jewelry. I saw a tiny gold charm in the shape of a triangle with a dove on it.

The triangle is the symbol for Alcoholics Anonymous, and the dove is the symbol of the Holy Spirit. I knew he had placed that charm in my path. I boarded the plane one of the happiest women in the world and surely the most blessed woman on earth.

I had been to the Sea of Galilee and had physically stepped out of the boat. Now I would return home and step out in faith. I would resign from my job and write his story of my life.

I started attending, yes, another Bible study. What a "study" in extremes my own life had become. During these days of crash-course learning groups, I was beginning to experience a wonderful sense of freedom! The freedom to be myself! The freedom to ask questions and not feel foolish! To share relevant things from my past and not be made to feel as though I was the "bad seed."

Sylvia, the woman who opened her home and did the teaching, was a gracious hostess and wonderful teacher. She spent hours on her computer planning lessons along with questions that provoked great discussions.

Most of the people in the group were church members and also attended our Life Group. We had become a family. We interacted, laughed, and shared a lot. We never left Sylvia's without an hour of fellowship over hot chocolate and homemade cake. Her finished basement had a pot belly stove, a full kitchen area, cozy chairs and comfy couches, all done in a country motif. This welcoming and inviting room immediately made me feel God's presence and the joy of being with others who were anxious to learn more about him!

How shocked I was at the end of the evening to be asked, "Roni, would you do the next week's Bible study?"

"Me?"

"Yes, you!" George responded.

"And we want to hear all the details of your trip to Israel," Sylvia said.

"Oh my goodness, I'd love to!" I said.

How sweet the sound of God's silent laughter as I glanced toward heaven and joined him in our private sentiment. That moment of knowing only he could have taken me from prison and set me on the path that would lead me to the Promised Land. And now he was giving me the opportunity to share with others my cherished memories of walking on his holy ground.

> As a prisoner for the Lord, then, I urge you to live a life worthy of the calling you have received. Be completely humble and gentle; be patient, bearing with one another in love. Make every effort

to keep the unity of the Spirit through the bond
of peace.

Ephesians 4:1–3 (NIV)

Sylvia is one of those rare people who can turn a few
grains of sand into pearls and a space beneath her basement stairs into a mini-library. Being an avid reader and
a new Christian added to my newfound hunger to learn
more about the Lord; I became engrossed by the wall of
Christian books with hundreds of intriguing titles.

"Sylvia, do you mind if I borrow a few?" I asked.

"Take whichever ones you want," she'd say with her
little Dutch accent.

One of the books I chose was *The Pursuit of God*.
In it, the author, A.W. Tozer, wrote, "The Bible is the
infallible declaration of God's mind for us, put into our
familiar human words."

What an intriguing thought, *infallible declaration of
God's mind.*

And if you call out for insight and cry aloud for
understanding, and if you look for it as for silver
and search for it as for hidden treasure.

Proverbs 2:3, 4 (NIV)

And there from under Sylvia's basement steps was
a hidden treasure, giving me another opportunity to see
more of the scriptures unfold and become real in my own
life.

Reading about the twelve apostles became another turning point in my walk with the Lord.

Growing up, I always thought of the apostles as being these perfect men. It never occurred to me that Jesus would choose the type of people he did.

I was still struggling to understand many things in the Bible. Someone suggested that I buy a few videos. I bought the complete book of Matthew and another one about Peter and Paul. They were worth the investment, as I better understood the scriptures with the visual of the movies and having been to Israel.

> Jesus went out and saw a tax collector by the name of Matthew sitting at his tax booth. "Follow me," Jesus said to him. And Matthew got up, left everything and followed him.
>
> Mark 2:14 (NIV)
>
> Then Matthew held a great banquet for Jesus at his house, and a large crowd of tax collectors and others were eating with them. But the Pharisees and the teachers of the law who belonged to their sect complained to His disciples, "Why do you eat and drink with tax collectors and 'sinners'?"
>
> Jesus answered them, "It is not the healthy who need a doctor, but the sick. I have not come to call the righteous, but sinners to repentance."
>
> Luke 5:29–31 (NIV)

From this scripture, we assume tax collectors were not the most honest people, especially since Matthew was dining with sinners.

My father worked for the Internal Revenue Service. His whole adult life he did income tax returns. He was as honest as the day is long. Matthew was skimming off the top; my father's clients pleaded with him to find more deductions so they'd get money back. Truly my father was a man of integrity, and that didn't sit well with many of his clients. So we see just the words tax collector had a bad reputation.

I would have better understood Jesus sitting with someone like my dad long before I could picture him sitting with the likes of Matthew.

It's such a powerful story. Jesus sitting with all these sinners, yet his reason for being with them made perfect sense. All I had to do was think back about my brother and know the doctor came to see him because he was sick. There would be no reason for the doctor to visit Patrick had he been healthy.

During this time, I was going into the women's county jail to lead AA meetings. Now I could better understand the reason for Jesus choosing people like me. As one of the greatest sinners, he was giving me the opportunity to tell my story and share my testimony. For people in recovery, we trust those who share in our common malady far more than someone who never knew the despair of addiction.

I can remember in grammar school learning the Beatitudes and having to memorize them word for word. Then, forty-five years later, I traveled to Israel and had the experience of sitting on the same hillside where Jesus preached this sermon. All of us from the group read those verses aloud. It was awesome.

And now, a few years later, I'm finding out who wrote the first book in the New Testament and who we have to thank for recording the Sermon on the Mount. It was Matthew.

I remember walking in the area of Caesarea-Philippi and thinking this was the same place where Jesus asked the apostles, "Who do you say I am?" Peter responded, "Thou art the Christ, the son of the living God!" (Matthew 16:15, 16 NIV).

For those of us who attended Catholic grammar school, we will never forget the story of Peter denying he knew Jesus, not once but three times.

> "But I have prayed for you, that your faith may not fail. And when you have turned back, strengthen your brothers," but Peter replied, "Lord, I am ready to go with you to prison and to death." Jesus answered, "I tell you, Peter before the rooster crows today, you will deny three times that you know me."
>
> Luke 22:32–34 (NIV)

One day, Peter is declaring Jesus to be the Christ, the son of the living God; and a short time later, he's denying that he even knows Jesus.

Still, Jesus named him Peter, which means rock. And Peter lived up to that name. He was the foundation the church was built on. Millions of people visit St. Peter's basilica every year.

> Also a dispute arose among them as to which of them was considered to be the greatest.
>
> Luke 22:24 (NIV)

Their imperfect humanness is summed up in that one verse.

Grown men acting as childish as many still do today. We always want to be the favorite or the greatest. We've all seen pictures of the Last Supper, and we look upon it with respect and reverence, and I laugh thinking that these men who I thought were so holy and so perfect were squabbling over who was going to sit at the right hand of Jesus. Who was the favorite?

And of course, we all know Judas was the traitor. The one who proclaimed his loyalty to Jesus but chose instead to betray Jesus for a mere thirty pieces of silver.

One of the most powerful scenes in the Bible is the Last Supper. Jesus already knows he's about to be betrayed. He knows all too well what lies ahead. And yet we read the following most mind-bending scripture.

> Silently! Jesus got up from the meal, took off his outer clothing, and wrapped a towel around his waist. After that, he poured water into a basin and began to wash his disciples' feet, then drying them with a towel.
>
> John 13:3, 4 (NIV)

He willingly becomes the servant to all these sinners.

Then we come to Paul, known as Saul before his conversion. Of all the people in the Bible, the story of Paul absolutely blew me away. We've all heard of Paul, and again, I always thought of him as one of the original apostles. Now I find out he never even met Jesus. He was persecuting and torturing Christians. He was very hostile to the Christian faith. He was on his way to

Damascus carrying documents authorizing him to seize the followers of Jesus and bring them back to face trial.

But here we see the greatest example of how different God's plans were and we just can't thwart his plans.

> As he neared Damascus on his journey, suddenly a light from heaven flashed around him. He fell to the ground and heard a voice say to him, "Saul, Saul, why do you persecute me?" "Who are you, Lord?" Saul asked. "I am Jesus, whom you are persecuting," he replied." Now get up and go into the city, and you will be told what you must do."
>
> Acts 9:3–6 (NIV)

From that moment on, he is called Paul.

I honestly felt I had been struck by the same light. That was such an eye-opener. The words Jesus spoke to Paul also applied to me. I had blamed everything on God. I may not have been persecuting Christians physically, but I sure was doing it verbally, and in so doing, I was also persecuting Jesus. This whole thing really shook my world, but in a good way.

Paul left his family and his heritage behind and did what the Lord told him to do.

In God's infinite wisdom, he chose the one man whose faith and belief we have to thank for the thousands of Christians in the world today. There was no one before him and no one since who could even hold a candle to this "world changer."

Just by using these few stories, we know Jesus's choice of disciples was deliberate and perfect.

They were amazingly similar to us. If we took them out of the Bible and placed them on any main street in

New Jersey today, they would be so like us we would see them as contemporaries.

For all who are reading this, I urge you to start reading the Bible. Not only will you be learning, you will find parts that will make you laugh. Just ponder the following scriptures.

> As Jesus and his disciples were on their way, he came to a village where a woman named Martha opened her home to him. She had a sister called Mary, who sat at the Lord's feet listening to what he said. But Martha was distracted by all the preparations that had to be made. She came to him and asked, "Lord, don't you care that my sister has left me to do the work by myself? Tell her to help me!"
>
> "Martha, Martha," the Lord answered, "you are worried and upset about many things, but only one thing is needed. Mary has chosen what is better, and it will not be taken away from her."
>
> Luke 11:38–42 (NIV)

Oh please! Which one of us hasn't done exactly what Martha did? How many times have we been in the kitchen preparing a meal all alone while our siblings, cousins, and kids are enjoying a relaxing afternoon watching football or playing games or just kicking back in the recliner?

I don't know that the Bible's intention is to be humorous, but I know for myself, I've discovered many verses that I could have inserted my own name in them, many times. I just love the last line; it sounds to me like Martha is demanding that Jesus tell Mary to help her. That is too funny.

Another great example is in one of Jesus's parables. Don't get the idea here that I'm any Bible scholar. It was only after I started attending Bible studies and the scriptures were explained to me in a way that made sense. The ones that I clearly remember are the ones that came alive in my own personal life.

The following verses tell us a story that is both strikingly fair and it can also be strikingly unfair.

> "For the kingdom of heaven is like a landowner who went out early in the morning to hire men to work in his vineyard. He agreed to pay them a denarius for the day and sent them into his vineyard. About the third hour he went out and saw others standing in the marketplace doing nothing. He told them, 'You also go and work in my vineyard, and I will pay you whatever is right.' So they went. He went out again about the sixth hour and the ninth hour and did the same thing. About the eleventh hour he went out and found still others standing around. He asked them, 'Why have you been standing here all day long doing nothing?'
>
> 'Because no one has hired us,' they answered.
>
> He said to them, 'You also go and work in my vineyard.'
>
> When evening came, the owner of the vineyard said to his foreman, 'Call the workers and pay them their wages, beginning with the last ones hired and going on to the first.'
>
> The workers who were hired about the eleventh hour came and each received a denarius. So when those came who were hired first, they expected to receive more. But each one of them also received a denarius. When they received it, they began to

grumble against the landowner. 'These men who were hired last worked only one hour,' they said, 'and you have made them equal to us who have borne the burden of the work and the heart of the day.'

But he answered one of them, 'Friend, I am not being unfair to you. Didn't you agree to work for a denarius? Take your pay and go. I want to give the man who was hired last the same as I gave you. Don't I have the right to do what I want with my own money? Or are you envious because I am generous?'"

Matthew 20:1–5 (NIV)

There are many times in our lives when we feel we've been cheated or shortchanged and we think it's not fair. But there is no denying the fact that the landowner did promise them a denarius and that's what they got. It was his money, and he could do with it as he pleased. And his last remark again could have my name in it; yes, Roni would be envious.

One lesson I took away with me after reading this and experiencing many such times is to stop comparing. Whoever said "all unhappiness is caused by comparison" knew what they were talking about.

ONLY BY GOD'S DIVINE INGENUITY

The grandest most significant event in all of human history—and God chose a woman? A prostitute! How remarkable.

> Early on the first day of the week, while it was still dark, Mary Magdalene went to the tomb and saw that the stone had been removed from the entrance.
>
> John 20:1 (NIV)

She ran to Simon Peter and told him that someone had taken the Lord out of the tomb. Mary returned to the tomb and stood outside crying. Turning around, she saw Jesus standing there but did not realize that it was Jesus.

He asked her why she was crying, and still she did not know it was him until he called her name.

"Mary." And she cried out in Aramaic, "Rabboni!" (which means teacher) (John 20:16 NIV).

Mary Magdalene went to the disciples with the news: "I have seen the Lord!"

In her book, *Mad Mary*, Liz Curtis Higgs writes the words Mary Magdalene was thinking after Jesus's death. "She would never hear his voice again, never hear his laugh. Never hear him say her name, Mary. Why hadn't she paid more attention the last time they were together?"

Was it coincidence that those thoughts were my exact thoughts regarding my brother?

I would never hear Patrick's voice again, never hear his laugh. Never hear him say my name. I would never hear another one of his sermons. How many times I wished I had listened more attentively.

Higgs noted, "No wonder Mary Magdalene's dawn meeting with her Savior among the garden shadows is considered 'the greatest recognition scene in all literature.'" She goes on to say Mary's story "begins with the darkest of all human misery and ends with the most glorious day in the history of the world."

In my search to find the verses that proclaim her iniquities, I could find none. This was a significant discovery. All my life, when I heard the name Mary Magdalene, it immediately triggered thoughts of a woman who was a prostitute.

I truly believe it is for that reason Jesus chose to appear to Mary Magdalene. He knew the truth about her, and he knew that her undeserved reputation would follow her for centuries to come.

Now, when I read these scriptures, I feel special and I feel loved. Jesus knows the truth about me. He understands me and knows what it is like to feel alone and wrongly accused. All I can say is "Amen" to the fact that Jesus does not judge us in the same manner the world judges us, and he forgives us in a way the world is incapable of forgiving.

> When Jesus rose early on the first day of the week, he appeared first to Mary Magdalene, out of whom he had driven seven demons.
>
> Mark 16:9 (NIV)

She was not the adulteress or the woman who poured perfume on Jesus's feet.

But Mary of Magdala had a deep love and reverent gratitude toward Jesus for driving away the demons that tortured her. She followed Jesus for three years as he went about preaching. She followed him all the way to the cross.

Like Mary Magdalene, I also have a deep love and reverent gratitude toward Jesus for driving away the demons that tortured me.

God shows a marked preference for "real" people over "good" people. Jesus said, "There will be more rejoicing in Heaven over one sinner who repents than over ninety-nine righteous persons who do not need to repent" (Luke 15:7 NIV).

We are all sinners saved by grace.

Their stories were *my story;* their lives were *my life.* From your average everyday housewife and mother, I became a liar, a cheat, an adulteress, and a thief. "Susie homemaker" and "Nancy nurse" evaded paying her taxes, was a blasphemer, and a drunk. I coveted. I lusted. I was prideful and envious.

Every time I attend an AA meeting, I speak to people just like those in the Bible. I look into the eyes of Mary Magdalene, Judas, Peter, Paul, King David, Bathsheba, and Solomon. They mirror my brokenness, my sinfulness, and my vulnerability.

As the great missionary Hudson Taylor said, "All God's giants were weak people."

How could we ever doubt the authenticity of the Bible, when those same stories and events continue today? Only the names and faces have changed.

Bible scholar Dr. James E. Gibson wrote, "The stories and sayings of the Bible have survived thousands of years, because generation upon generation found in them a *practical wisdom.* It was a wisdom that helped to solve everyday problems, as well as to resolve theological and spiritual issues."

I was beginning to see that God is not a punishing God. Quite the reverse—he wants me to stop punishing myself.

But real life does have a way of creeping back in. Mother's Day was fast approaching.

Eric called me a week before and invited me to come into New York on Mother's Day and they'd take me out to dinner. I graciously accepted and thought, *This is awesome. Now I have something to look forward to. No more fretting!*

Saturday evening, when I returned home, there was a message. He was sorry he had to cancel; he was going out of town. Not even a twenty-four-hour notice.

A very deep sadness was the only way I could describe my feelings at that moment. I don't know whether that was good or bad or whether I had passed the test or not. No anger, no hurt, there was nothing, and that's what I found to be so disheartening. No mother should ever have to experience the likes of such numbness that she is forced to betray every feeling she ever had for her own child.

The following morning in church, an unexpected lump in my throat caught me off guard. The sermon about mothers was wonderful. I asked myself, *Where do I fit in?* The daughter who recently lost a mother she never felt love from and the mother of a son who didn't have time for her. I would never have made it through that day had I not felt God hugging me in his arms.

A few days later, I was in California with Chad, ecstatic as I watched him present his final thesis and a few days later walk up to receive his diploma from the Southern California Institute of Architecture. It was a very heartfelt and emotional moment. He never at any point during his illness wavered in his determination to complete his college education. Only he and I knew the hardships he had endured and the obstacles he had overcome to reach the end of this long and arduous journey.

He had made me a special Mother's Day card with a note thanking me for being there to watch him present his thesis and attend his graduation. I wouldn't have missed it for anything.

It had been a wonderful, wonderful trip. I had the opportunity to visit with friends and go to some meetings I used to attend. Chad and I went to the new Getty Museum and to the movies and out to dinner. I had an awesome time with him.

Just like the Lord tells us, "Come to me all you who are heavy of burden and I will give you rest." He has kept his word.

The first message I received when I arrived home was from a woman by the name of Greta.

"Hi, Roni, my name is Greta. I saw your name on the bulletin board at the Westfield Tennis Club. We're looking for another player. If you're still interested, please give me a call."

This was the icing on the cake. I had not played tennis for years and longed to get back into the game. I called her immediately, and the following week, I became a regular in their Tuesday night games.

Hazel Lee wrote, "I held a moment in my hand, brilliant as a star, fragile as a flower, a shiny sliver out of one hour. I dropped it carelessly. O God! I knew not I held an opportunity."

This was a poignant reminder of all the moments I had carelessly dropped, the opportunities lost. God in his graciousness was replacing each one of my lost opportunities with a new and better one. I could see God's ways more clearly than ever in the past. Even in something as simple as playing tennis, he saw to it that I found women my age to join with, but even more personal was his partnering me with Greta. She and I became good friends through our belief in the Lord. So you see God is even on the tennis courts.

Ten days after I returned from California, I heard from Eric. He was walking home from work and called me from his cell phone.

"Hi, Mom, how are you?" he asked.

"I'm fine, and yourself?"

"Listen, I can't talk too long; I just wanted to let you know I changed jobs," he informed me.

"Congratulations!"

I already knew about his job change. That was old news that he was finally getting around to share with me.

"I'll call you when I have more time to talk," he said.

A few months later, Eric suggested that he, Kim, and I sit and have a talk. He felt what took place in regard to my mother should be discussed.

"Eric, I did everything possible to make my mother happy, and I took excellent care of her," I said. "There is no need for any discussion. She's gone."

I was pleasant but firm.

There were not going to be any confrontations or tit-for-tat debates about what they thought. From experience, I knew any further discourse would be like adding oxygen to a smoldering fire. It was not going to be easy, but I had to let the fire burn out. That was a zenith moment for me! It was over.

> It is also not our job to defend ourselves against criticism. "My work is too important to stop now and … visit with you."
>
> Nehemiah 6:3 (CEV)

To paraphrase what Tozer had written: From the moment Abraham first picked up his son, Isaac, he had become a love slave. The baby represented everything sacred to his father's heart: the promises of God, the covenants that had been made, the hopes of years of waiting, and the dreams of the future. As Abraham watched Isaac grow into manhood, the heart of the old man was knit closer and closer with the life of his son, till the relationship bordered upon the perilous. It was then that God stepped in to save both father and son from the consequences of that obsessive love.

> "Take your son, your only son, Isaac, whom you love, and go to the region of Moriah. Sacrifice him there as a burnt offering on one of the mountains I will tell you about."
>
> Genesis 22:2 (NIV)

Like Abraham, I would (figuratively) place my obsessive love, my compulsive behaviors, everything that stood between myself and God, and place them on the altar and pray for the strength to leave them there.

RESPECTFUL SILENCE

"Who is this that darkens my counsel with words without knowledge?"

Job 38:2 (NIV)

Job and his friends had exhausted their words of complaint, explanation, and condemnation. Then God appeared as a voice and spoke to Job.

Job was immediately reduced to "Respectful Silence."

The book of Job is a compelling compilation of dramas with deeper meanings below what is really taking place. The significance is just the beginning of knowing the power God bestows on those who trust him. For two years, I asked the same question over and over again, determined to find that one answer that would satisfy me and bring an end to my longsuffering. I had to know, what kind of a mother would banish her own daughter?

For weeks following Patrick's death, the same question would arise, "How did he endure the pain and suffering without question or complaint?"

It was not the silence of speech that I struggled to understand. It was the aura of his silence. His acceptance of the solitude, every day and every night. It became an obsession. No doubt, my obsession was brought on by fear. What if that happened to me? Not a very admirable obsession. Still, I had to know what my brother's secret was.

It wasn't natural. It wasn't normal to go through what he did without some bitterness or resentment, or "why me?"

I remember asking, "Patrick, has your illness caused you to lose any faith or to become angry with God?"

His expression is still vivid, with that look of disbelief. "No!"

I had no trouble reading his lips.

Patrick loved being a priest; he loved people and giving sermons. In return, he was very much loved and respected. Expending days and hours, along with pondering numerous books, he had the ability to extract the precise number of words so that he became known as the priest of three-minute sermons.

"It's hard to keep people's attention," he would respond.

He loved kids and would combine humor with stories of *Snoopy* or *E.T.* at the same time, skillfully interspersing scriptures.

A friend and fellow seminarian visited Patrick at the hospital. The family joined in as Father Joel said mass. Patrick, fully awake, received communion. He passed away one week later on Sunday. The Lord gave him rest on the "seventh" day.

Patrick had a faith that made me say, "I believe no more, at last I see."

Silence has surely been the thread throughout this book. After reading the book of Job, I saw the importance of silence, and I found the answer to my first haunting question. How did Patrick endure his suffering? As a Catholic priest he no doubt was familiar with Job. I had my answer. Patrick never questioned God, he never complained.

It was in that discovery that I found the answer to my second question: How could my mother kick me out?

Suddenly it seemed so simple. Stop asking why. Only God could give me complete peace of mind without ever giving me an answer. *Just be still.*

Samuel Beckett wrote, "We can speak using words to evoke the hollowness and perimeters of our intelligence, words that express the paradox of not having the capacity and yet having the need."

As the wounded daughter, I had stretched my account of hurt and unfairness to the extreme, before I could admit the truth of that statement.

Legend tells of a woman who came to the river Styx to be ferried across to the land of the departed spirits. Charos, the ferryman, offers her a magic potion, which can cause her to forget the life she is leaving and all its sorrows. In the end, the woman leaves the potion untasted, choosing to remember life's pains and sorrows and failures rather than forget its joys, its triumphs, and its loves. Sorrow and joy belong together. They are precious experiences, which deepen understanding and give meaning to life.

It sounds wonderful to take a sip and forget all the grief and pain, but that would mean forgetting the happy marriage I had for twenty years, the two miracles I gave birth to, the friends and family and all the good memories.

But the saddest part would have been missing the blessed opportunity to see Patrick and I become like-minded through God's miraculous gift of *silence*.

As the weeks continued to zoom by, my peace and contentment soared. Every day, I walked through this marvelous labyrinth with no fear of getting lost and no need to worry about where it would lead. Every pathway took me to some new, exciting place.

For months, the journey led me to new friends and new spiritual experiences. Another road took me to greater heights of learning through the retreats and Bible studies. Another path took me to Israel.

Upon my return from Israel, I hungered to learn about his Word. This led to a most fascinating curiosity about Jesus's disciples. Now God was opening another pathway, and I was hearing about people whose lives changed history. They were the poorest of the poor but knew contentment and peace beyond anything I ever dreamed possible. And *silence* was their cornerstone. No bullhorns, no shouting, and no begging. They just did the next right thing because they knew it was God's will.

I remember the night Princess Diana died in a car accident. The news of that tragic accident sent shock waves through the world. You could not turn on the television without hearing the details. A few days later, I was at a meeting where a friend of mine, Lynn, came in a few minutes late and whispered to me, "Mother Teresa died." I was too embarrassed to ask, "Who is Mother Teresa?" They had both died within a day or so, yet there was very little coverage of Mother Teresa.

Two years later, I found a copy of a newspaper clipping among Patrick's belongings. It was a very short article about Mother Teresa written by Robert Fulghum. I was shocked by what this one woman accomplished, also by the fact that I had never heard of her. I was too immersed in myself to take notice of some stooped woman from India. This woman had received a Nobel Peace Prize. Mother Teresa of India, servant of the poor and sick and dying. This nun who held more power than any pope or president or king. She held the most powerful and invincible weapon against the evils of this world: the caring heart.

In their book entitled *Falling in Love with Jesus*, Dee Brestin and Kathy Troccoli wrote:

> Mother Teresa tells of her experience while visiting a nursing home here in the States. She asked the nun in charge: "Why do these people, who have every comfort here—why are they looking toward the door? Why are they not smiling? I am so used to seeing the smiles on our people even the dying ones smile."
>
> And Sister said, "These people are expecting— they are hoping—that a son or a daughter will come to visit them. They are hurt because they are forgotten."

As I thought back to Mother's Day and not hearing from my son, I felt the pain of the very people Mother Teresa described. I didn't have to be in that nursing home to see the look on their faces. I saw it every time I looked in the mirror. I'd had that look on my face for a year now, waiting for a call from my son. A call I knew would never come.

In another book written about Mother Teresa, *A Simple Path,* she is quoted as saying: "I always begin my prayer in silence. For it is in the silence of the heart that God speaks. God is the friend of silence—we need to listen to God because it's not what we say but what he says to us and through us that matters."

Mother Teresa knew it was her experience of the *silence* of God that brought her close to all who have struggled with faith. She was emphatic in her response— cling to God regardless of the circumstances. Where it got her was into the will of God. Day by day, she did what God asked. Some would say she was successful. But her response to those who thought of her as being successful was, "God doesn't call us to be successful. He calls us to be faithful." One of her favorite expressions was, "If we are faithful, we will become something beautiful for God."

What a magnificent summation of what she herself became, "something beautiful for God." She was someone filled with love for the Father.

Is silence all but extinct in our modern society? Who can hear him when he speaks?

BLESS YOU, PRISON

In recent years, my heart has been squeezed in another direction, and the flow has reversed itself. It has brought me to God with the blessing of a relationship with his Son. I feel now that I am in the right place. Allowing the Lord to lead me has made my life so much easier and joyful. I'd never known contentment or security until I let go and let God.

The novelist Aleksandr Solzhenitsyn spent ten years in prison as punishment for a careless remark he made about Stalin in a personal letter. However, after his release, he wrote, "Bless you, prison, for having been in my life. For it was there I discovered, the meaning of earthly existence lies, not as we have grown used to thinking, in prospering, but in the development of the soul."

Though innocent, Solzhenitsyn spent time in prison; there he found God. Through many poor choices I too spent time in prison; there the seed was planted.

When Brad and I moved to California, we had high hopes and good intentions. We were excited about our new adventure, the sunny skies, and warm weather. We bought a home. Our sons were doing very well in school. I was working in a wonderful hospital, and Brad had a good job. He and I thought alike—we had the same dreams. We began going to church, looking forward to breakfast at the Pancake House afterward. We enrolled the kids in catechism classes. We took them to Magic Mountain and Knott's Berry Farm. Both of them loved playing baseball, and for years, they played in Little League. Brad often helped coach at their games. He took the kids rock climbing the weekend I studied for my nursing exams. We took them on camping trips. Chad was a Boy Scout. To our amazement, we learned that snow does fall on California, and it was there in the mountains of San Bernardino that we took the boys skiing the first year we were there. We were a real family and never doubted that we would grow old together.

Who could have imagined that when I returned to New Jersey after twenty years, I would disembark from the plane as a recovering alcoholic, an ex-offender, and without Brad? One might say I was in the wrong place at the wrong time, but such was not the case. I was there because I was not a totally good person and my heart got squeezed in the wrong direction.

Sixteen years ago, during a Sunday service at Avenal State Prison in California, where I was serving time, a preacher described his struggle with drugs. For years he tried to get clean, but he kept relapsing, and each time his addiction got worse. "In my blackest and most desperate moment, I stepped into an empty room," he said. "There I proceeded to put on a pair of boxing gloves and

I boxed with the devil. I punched and I punched until Satan couldn't get up and then I walked out of that room and never used drugs again."

Ten years later, that seed burst forth and blossomed. That story unknowingly had been embedded in the recesses of my mind and had lain dormant until the moment I would need to put on the boxing gloves and box with the devil. I have worn those gloves many times and often for long, grueling hours. My temptation in recent years was not to run back to alcohol or drugs; instead, I wanted to unleash my tongue and let my family know how much they hurt me. But I knew I would never reach the moment when I could do it without all the pent-up anger and venom dripping from my tongue. I will never be a totally good person. But with the mental and visual acuity of the story that preacher told, I learned the greatest lesson of all. To give in to the enemy would have cost me everything.

> Everyone should be quick to listen, slow to speak and slow to become angry, for man's anger does not bring about the righteous life that God desires.
>
> James 1:19–20 (NIV)

For the past five years, I've been going into the women's county jail to conduct AA meetings. I've trained with Chuck Colson's Prison Ministry, and today I choose to return to the men's and women's facilities. I love sharing my testimony of hope. It is an honor to give God all the glory.

For a year now, I've been going in with a team every Friday night to the men's prison. God has blessed me in ways I could never convey in words. One of the people on the team is a Roman Catholic nun. If ever there was a replica of Mother Teresa, it is Sister Rosemary. She is eighty-two years young and has a love for the inmates that I could only wish to have. Nothing else matters to her but the time she spends with these people. When we pick her up, she is loaded down with canvas bags and briefcases overflowing with booklets and pictures to hand out. She spends hours cutting and pasting and copying. Every week, she handwrites another lesson from *The Purpose Driven Life* study guide. Her enthusiasm and childlike excitement is contagious, and her gratitude for the opportunity to spend time with the inmates is stunning.

The men who show up on Friday night you would not want to meet in a dark alley. But they immediately become quiet, anxious to talk to Sister Rosemary and to ask questions about her love of the Lord, which is evident through her love for these men and women.

> The Spirit of the Sovereign Lord is on me, because the Lord has anointed me to preach good news to the poor. He has sent me to bind up the brokenhearted, to proclaim freedom for the captives and release from darkness for the prisoners.
>
> Isaiah 61:1 (NIV)

I pray that my testimony will change one person's life as completely as that preacher's testimony changed mine.

Bless you, prison, for having been in my life, for it was there I found my Prince of Peace!

GOD CONTINUES TO SPEAK TO ME IN SILENCE

> Pilate again asked Jesus, "Aren't you going to answer? See how many things they are accusing you of." But Jesus still made no reply, and Pilate was amazed.
>
> Mark 15:4–5 (NIV)

The above scripture reading was the defining moment that changed my life forever. It is a powerful illustration set before us in a spellbinding visual. *Jesus made no reply.*

It is impossible for any human being to perfectly express the feelings of one's heart. The more we attempt to explain our feelings, the less power our words have. Sometimes *silence* is the only expression we have.

Remembering Patrick sitting with his head resting in his hands, I believe these were his times of divine commune with Jesus. Those were the moments he was closest to heaven, and through his weakness, the Lord gave him the strength to endure the many days and nights in silence.

Hudson Taylor, a missionary to China, scrawled on a piece of paper as he neared the end of his life: "I am so weak that I cannot work. I cannot read the Bible. I cannot even pray. I can only lie still in God's arms like a child, and trust."

I recalled my family telling me how peaceful Patrick looked when he went into the coma. Surely my brother was resting in the arms of his loving Father, and for five days, it was just the two of them. What a glorious thought!

I know today that all my experiences served as a passage of preparation leading me to that one moment when I could fully embrace the miraculous juncture where Patrick and I would meet. While I am still traveling my path to the Lord, Patrick's path took him home to be with the Lord.

As I draw closer to God, he embraces me. He serves me. He loves me. And he makes me feel as though I am his beloved child. He converses with me without the need to mention my sinful past. I know peace beyond measure. I know joy. I know contentment.

Thank you, Patrick, for being a living example of a faith that I too have embraced and which has guaranteed that we will meet again someday in that glorious place called heaven.

Before his accusers, Jesus stood silent. On the cross Jesus forgave. On the third day, Jesus rose.

Now it is my turn to be silent. It is my turn to forgive. It is time for me to live the life Jesus died for me to have and to fulfill the plans God has for me.

Through my brother's silence, I heard his greatest sermon.

Through Jesus's silence, I learned how to be still in the face of accusations.

Through the Holy Spirit's silence, I have been strengthened and comforted.

Through God's silence, I have found the greatest love of all.